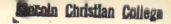

Psychology for Church Leaders Series

MAN IN TRANSITION

The Psychology of Human Development

Gary R. Collins

CREATION HOUSE
Carol Stream, Illinois 60187

FIRST EDITION

Library of Congress Catalog Card Number: 79-163763

To

My Mother and Dad

ACKNOWLEDGMENTS

For permission to reprint excerpts in this book, acknowledgment is made to the following publishers:

The Atlantic Monthly—for excerpts from Mary Gonzales, "A Vote for Student Protest," Copyright © 1965, by The Atlantic Monthly Company, Boston, Mass. Reprinted with permission.

Basic Books, Inc.—for excerpts from T. Lidz, *The Person: His Development Throughout the Life Cycle,* 1968; and from Lois B. Murphy and Associates, *Personality in Young Children,* 1956.

The Bobbs-Merrill Company, Inc.—for excerpts from H. H. Remmers and D. A. Radler, *The American Teenager,* Copyright © 1957, by H. H. Remmers; reprinted by permission of the publisher.

Christianity Today—for excerpts from H. Lindsell, "Sex, SIECUS and the Schools," January 30, 1970. Copyright © 1970 by *Christianity Today;* reprinted by permission.

Eternity—for excerpts from E. Towns, "The Church and the Single Adult," October, 1968; reprinted by permission.

Harper & Row, Publishers, Inc.—for excerpts from A. Gesell and F. L. Ilg, *Child Development,* 1949.

McGraw-Hill Book Company—for excerpts from E. Hurlock, *Child Development.* Copyright © 1959, by Elizabeth Hurlock. Used with permission of McGraw-Hill Book Company.

National Sunday School Association—for excerpts from R. B. Zuck and G. A. Getz, *Christian Youth: An In-Depth Study,* 1968. Copyright © 1968, by National Sunday School Association.

Pastoral Psychology—for excerpts from articles by E.M . Pattison and J. A. Knight.

Prentice-Hall, Inc.—for excerpts from K. C. Garrison, *Psychology of Adolescence,* 6th ed., Copyright © 1965; and T. A. Harris, *Counseling The Serviceman and His Family,* Copyright © 1968.

Random House, Inc.—for excerpts from L. K. Frank, *On The Importance of Infancy,* Copyright © 1966; and L. J. Stone and J. Church, *Childhood and Adolescence,* 2nd. ed., Copyright © 1968.

Saturday Review—for excerpts from J. Kagan, "His Struggle for Identity," December 7, 1968. Copyright © 1968, Saturday Review Inc.

CONTENTS

PREFACE

This book is the first in a series written specifically for church leaders and for those who will become church leaders. Pastors, missionaries, Sunday school teachers, Christian education directors, lay leaders and theological Students—among others—often realize that psychological findings can be applicable to the work of the church, but most of these leaders lack the time and professional competence to keep abreast of the field of psychology and to determine what is applicable and what is not. The present volume (and those which follow in the "Psychology for Church Leaders" series) seeks to summarize the basic principles and latest findings from the field of psychology and to present these in a way that will be meaningful to church leaders who are not professional psychologists and who may have little or no background in psychology. *The book is not meant to be a comprehensive introduction to the whole field of developmental psychology. Instead, this book and the ones that follow are limited to those psychological conclusions which, in the author's opinion, have direct or indirect application to the problems and work of the church.* In many cases, the practical applications are explicitly stated.

The decision to write these books originated, so far as I can tell, from my perspectives as a psychologist, my commitment to a conservative theological position, my experiences as a seminary professor and my conclusions after talking to numerous church leaders at conferences around the country. The science of psychology has much that can be of practical value to Christian workers, but there are relatively few books which are sympathetic to biblical truths, which reflect the latest findings of contemporary psychology, which are free of complicated jargon and which show explicitly how psychology can be applied to the work of the church. In writing the present volume, I have tried to meet these needs.

The preparation of any book involves more people than the author. As always, my wife Julie gave constant encouragement as I worked on the manuscript. She made innumerable helpful suggestions about what I had written, prodded when prodding was needed, and patiently encouraged as I worked. My colleague, Curtis Wennerdahl, along with a number of alert students, read and perceptively criticized portions of the manuscript. Mrs. Ronald Gifford typed and retyped most of the chapters, but she was helped at times by several other secretaries who deciphered my writing and endured my frequent editing. My graduate assistant, John Hochevar, spent many hours proof-reading, tracking down information, and helping with the index. To all of these people I am sincerely grateful.

Psychologists and others have clearly shown that a person's personality and interests are molded by a number of early experiences. My parents, Mr. and Mrs. H. A. Collins of Hamilton, Ontario, guided me through my early years with a firm but kind discipline, teaching me the value of study and further education. As I went through school they encouraged but never pushed. They immediately accepted my wife as one of the family and subsequently have shown themselves to be excellent grandparents. It is to them that this book is gratefully and affectionately dedicated.

Gary R. Collins

Mundelein, Illinois
May 1, 1971

Chapter One

PSYCHOLOGY AND THE CHURCH LEADER

What is man really like? Why does he behave like he does? What are his needs? Why can't he get along with his fellows? How does he learn? Why does he kill or steal or become a mental patient?

Questions such as these have concerned men for centuries. The psalmist asked about the nature of man (Psalm 8:4); Aristotle and the ancient philosophers debated about man's behavior; St. Augustine was interested in how people think; and subsequent generations of philosophers, theologians, and others have sought to understand who man is and why he acts as he does. Most of these thinkers have used a method known as *armchair theorizing*. Sometimes on the basis of a few observations, and sometimes as the result of reasoning alone, sweeping conclusions were made about the complexities of human behavior.

Psychology as a discipline rejected armchair theorizing and has sought instead to apply the scientific method to these age-old questions about man. While the attempt to understand human behavior is very old, the science of psychology is relatively young. Most historians trace its beginnings to the year 1879 when a German named Wilhelm Wundt founded the first psychological laboratory in Leipzig. Since that time literally thousands of professional psychologists have studied the complexities of human behavior in an attempt to discover what man is like and how he can be changed.

11

Today, *psychology is defined as a science, and an art, which studies the directly observable behavior of men and animals and the less directly observable feelings, thoughts, motives, and self-concepts that cause or accompany such behavior.* The purpose of psychology is to understand, predict, and control the behavior of men and animals. Psychology is a science because it attempts to apply precise scientific techniques—in so far as this is possible—to the study of behavior. Psychologists are concerned with both the behavior which is directly observable—such as a man's actions or words—and the behavior which is less easily observed—such as a man's feelings and thoughts.[1] While psychology is primarily a science, it is also an art which involves the skillful application of psychological principles to the individual problems of people who are having difficulty in their personal adjustment, in their marriages, with their schoolwork, or with their businesses. Both in the laboratory and in applied situations psychologists attempt to understand, predict, and control behavior. It will be noted that psychologists are interested in the behavior of both men and animals. Large numbers of psychologists work only with animals, but for the most part, this aspect of psychology will be overlooked in the following pages.

Like most modern fields of learning, psychology is so complex that the discipline has been broken down into a number of specialties. The specialties that interest more psychologists than any other are *clinical* and *counseling* psychology. These are concerned with understanding and helping people who have problems. The clinical-counseling psychologist administers psychological tests, counsels with groups and individuals, and does research concerning normal and abnormal behavior. Clinical psychology can help the church leader to recognize, understand, and deal with the problems of church members. *School and educational* psychology deals with the problems and challenges of education. Although psychologists in this specialty spend much of their time testing problem children and making recommendations to teachers, school psychologists also conduct remedial reading programs, and study instructional techniques, curriculum development, and other educational issues. This specialty is growing (Bardon, 1968) [2] and should have something to say to the church leader who is interested in religious instruction.

Experimental psychology is concerned with the physiological basis of behavior and with the details of perception, motivation, learning, and emotion. *Social* psychology is concerned with human behavior in groups. Topics like leadership, prejudice, group pressure, attitudes, and communication, concern the social psychologist. *Developmental* psychology studies the behavior of individuals as they develop through life. Since the focus is on typical normal behavior at various age periods, and the potential problems that we all encounter as we grow older, the findings of this field can have great relevance to the work of the church, and are discussed in detail in the pages that follow.

These major subdivisions within psychology are not the only fields of specialization. Industrial psychology, military psychology, consumer psychology, philosophical psychology, engineering psychology, abnormal psychology, parapsychology (the study of ESP and similar phenomena) and more recently "black psychology" are among the fields of specialization. The profession is rapidly expanding and there are now over 30,000 professional psychologists in the United States and Canada.

Misconceptions About Modern Psychology

Within its relatively short history, psychology has become one of the most popular fields of study in institutions of higher education. Very frequently, however, students enroll in psychology courses only to be disappointed when they discover that psychology is something other than what they had expected. Regrettably, a number of misconceptions have developed and given psychology a false "public image." Among these false ideas are the following:

Psychology is just common sense

Psychologists—like sociologists, writers of literary works, lawyers, pastors, and others—seek to observe behavior with as much accuracy as possible. Some of the findings of psychological research have demonstrated experimentally what people have known for years to be "common sense." In these cases, psychology and common sense arrive at the same conclusions. In other situations, however, psychological findings are very different from popularly accepted conclusions. Many people, for example, believe that highly intelligent people are often sickly and social misfits, that intelligence is determined mainly by heredity, or that the "mentally ill" are unable to carry on logical conversations. Some people still believe that "blondes are dumb," that people with red hair have violent tempers, or that people with protruding chins are aggressive. These ideas, which to some people might be common sense, have all been studied psychologically and shown to be false. Psychology, therefore, cannot be passed off as "just common sense."

Psychology and psychologists are anti-religious

While this misconception is disappearing, there are still many people who believe that psychology is a God-hating subject. Rather than being *anti*-religious, however, psychology is *non*-religious. Most psychologists have tended to shrug off religion as being of no concern to the science which studies human behavior. The Christian psychologist, of course, believes differently. He recognizes that all truth comes from God. The Bible is the direct and authoritative revelation of God to man, but the Bible is not a psychology

14

textbook. God in His wisdom has permitted man to discover a great deal about himself and the world through the methods of science. Thus the Christian psychologist seeks to determine what, in the field of psychology, is consistent with the biblical teaching.

Psychology is the study of the mind

When the early American psychologists declared the mind "off limits" as a topic for psychological study, they did much for the advancement of their discipline. In popular speech, the term "mind" is used in different ways. It appears to be synonymous with memory ("I'll keep this in mind"), quality of thinking ("he has a good mind"), insanity ("he's out of his mind"), intention and determination ("I have a mind to go"), obedience ("mind your parents"), and similarity of opinion ("we are of one mind"). Often we talk of the mind as if it were something which we possess—like a brain. Because of these different ways in which the word "mind" is used, it would be hard to define this term accurately and precisely. To study such an elusive concept would be difficult, if not impossible. Psychologists have decided, instead, to study behavior.

Psychology is wierd and mysterious

When a psychologist is introduced in a social group, people sometimes feel uncomfortable and guarded. Apparently many feel that the psychologist can read people's thoughts and feelings in some kind of magical and mysterious way. While it may be helpful, at times, to have this ability, psychologists can no more read minds than can the pastor or family doctor. The psychologist's training often teaches him to be an accurate observer of behavior and to be sensitive to people's thinking and feeling, but there is nothing magical or mysterious about modern psychology.

15

Undoubtedly, one of the reasons for this misconception is that some people equate psychology with such practices as palmistry (the attempt to analyze character and predict the future from the lines on the palm of one's hand), astrology ("reading the stars"), phrenology (the analysis of character by examining the shape of the skull), and crystal ball gazing. In spite of the recent popularity of these techniques, most psychologists consider all of these to be pseudo-sciences (*pseudo* is a term meaning "false"). They have no basis in fact, although their practitioners are often very convincing. This is primarily because these fortune tellers are astute observers of human behavior and because their predictions are often vague and general enough to be highly probable (e.g., "You will have sadness during the coming year").

Psychology and the Church

On his recent retirement from the faculty of Andover-Newton Theological School, Walter Houston Clark described his career as a psychologist with an interest in religion. "Finding positions where I could teach the psychology of religion...has always been a chore," he wrote. Modern psychologists are not curious about religion and "neglectful...of the influence religion has...in human personality and human history. Since the time of William James (who in addition to his famous textbook, wrote a very influential book on religious experience), the psychological study of religion has fallen on dull days. In our day, its prestige has gradually begun to revive, but the conventional psychologist still tends to observe it warily as a subject that he is not quite sure belongs in his field" (1968).

This view is not hard to understand when one considers the history of psychology. In 1913 an American psychologist named John B. Watson founded the movement known as behaviorism. Watson (1967) believed that concepts like

16

"mind," "conscience" and "will" were vague and perhaps even non-existent. Certainly, they could not be measured, and thus they could not be studied scientifically. The behaviorists wanted instead to make psychology a science like physics and chemistry. To do this, they concluded that psychology must discard all consideration of subjective experiences and devote itself to the study of actual behavior—the kinds of actions that were plainly visible. If a behavior could not be observed, it was cast aside as being of no concern to psychology. Watson acknowledged that people had thoughts, but he believed that these were simply a form of talking to oneself. The small movements of the vocal chords which were supposed to accompany and indicate thinking, he concluded, would eventually be observable by scientific instruments. Emotions were not thought of as "feelings," but rather as glandular reactions which could be observed and measured.

Behaviorism was quickly accepted by experimental psychology and molded the future of psychological research. Since religious experience could not be observed and studied by scientific tools, the behaviorists concluded that anything concerned with religion was completely out of their field and of no interest to psychologists.

In the meantime, religion was also being rejected by clinical psychologists, but for different reasons. In Freud's writings, religion was the second most popular topic, but Freud was very critical of religion. He called it a universal neurosis—something like a narcotic that helps unstable people to endure life. Doctrine, Freud believed, was an illusion which hopefully would disappear as society matured and as science progressed (Freud, 1927). Many clinicians accepted Freud's conclusions and rejected religion as a topic for serious psychological study.

It is not surprising that church leaders reacted against these attitudes, so much so that even today many Christians are hostile toward psychology and skeptical of its influence. But a change is taking place. During the past few decades, psychologists have begun to show a much more sympathetic attitude toward religion. Many have come to realize that in order to understand behavior, the spiritual influences in a person's life cannot be ignored or explained away. Several former presidents of the American Psychological Association have even published books on religious topics (Allport, 1951; Meehl, 1958; Mowrer, 1961).

It is from within the church, however, that interest in the psychological study of religion has received its greatest impetus. In the early 1920's a pastor named Anton Boisen was hospitalized as a mental patient. When he was released, Boisen concluded that as part of their training, seminary students should have the opportunity of working with mental patients. Thus, in the summer of 1925 four theological students came to a state hospital in Massachusetts where they worked as attendants during the day and held seminars with Boisen in the evening (Boisen, 1936; Hall, 1968).

From modest beginnings such as this, a field known as "pastoral psychology" developed. Today, this is an important subject in the training of seminary students. Pastoral psychology has developed as *a discipline which examines psychological research and insights, evaluates these from a theological and biblical perspective, and attempts to determine how these can apply to the work of pastors and other church leaders.*

Most leaders in the pastoral psychology movement are of a theologically liberal persuasion. Within recent years, however, a few conservatives have become interested in this field and are attempting to determine how psychology is related to the Scriptures and how it can be relevant to the work of the local church.

Why Study Psychology?

Many of the findings and insights of psychology are directly applicable to the work of the church. Because of this, Christian leaders and theological students stand to profit from an understanding of psychological methods and conclusions. Specific reasons why church men and women should study psychology include the following:

A familiarization with psychology contributes to self-understanding

Students who enroll in psychology courses with the hope of understanding themselves better and solving their problems, are often disappointed. It is usually very difficult to recognize our own weaknesses or to see how our behavior can change. Jesus pointed this out when, in the sermon on the mount, He stated that it is much easier to analyze the failings of others than to see personal faults (Matthew 7:3-5). In spite of these difficulties, however, the perceptive student of psychology should be able to develop some increased understanding of his thoughts and actions. There are common ways in which we all react to frustration, for example, and the study of psychology should teach us something about our individual prejudices, emotions, and personality characteristics. Greater self-understanding is often accompanied by increased ability to get along with others. This is a worthy goal for all men—whether or not they are church leaders.

A familiarization with psychology contributes to a better understanding of others

One of the major goals of psychology is the understanding of human behavior. By studying this subject, the church leader can learn to observe other people more objectively and to develop an alertness to some of the possible causes of their behavior.

This increased understanding can apply to behavior that is abnormal and to that which is normal. By developing an alertness to the characteristics of "mental illness," for example, it is possible to detect and deal with problems in the early stages of their development. The Christian worker is also able to deal more effectively with parishioners when he observes and understands such normal events as the little child's fear of strangers, the adolescent's social awkwardness and concern about dating, the questioning attitudes of college students, the adjustment reactions of newlyweds or middle-aged adults, the reactions to grief, or the difficulties faced by healthy and active people who because of age are required to retire from their jobs.

The danger always exists, however, that beginning psychology students will become overly impressed with their new knowledge. Sometimes these students begin "analyzing" the behavior of their friends, relatives, and others. This, of course, is not always appreciated by the people who are being analyzed! The student must recognize, therefore, that human behavior is complex and its causes are multitudinous. While a familiarization with psychological findings increases one's understanding of behavior, we must use extreme caution in arbitrarily assigning "causes" and labels to what we observe. Most psychologists are very critical of newspaper columnists who answer letters by giving advice on personal matters. This criticism stems from the belief that information contained in letters is so limited and selective that it is impossible to determine accurately any real cause of the problem or to give sound advice. The same is often true of a student who, with limited knowledge and skill, becomes overly enthusiastic about "playing psychologist" with his friends.

A familiarization with psychology contributes to counseling effectiveness

In spite of the warning given in the above paragraph, it must be recognized that church leaders *are* involved in counseling. While it is possible that "a little knowledge is a dangerous thing," it is also true that in many cases some knowledge is better than no knowledge at all. More people take their problems to the church than to any other source

20

of help. For this reason the pastor and other church workers should have some skills in dealing with the problems of parishioners. Psychology can contribute to the development of these skills.

A familiarization with psychology contributes to the prevention of problems

The Christian church has both a remedial and a preventative task. We must assist people who have developed personal problems and need help in dealing with existing difficulties, but where possible, we should also attempt to prevent the occurence of problems. By discussing vocational and sexual concerns with teenagers, by warning high school seniors of the problems that they might face in college, by counseling with engaged couples, by preaching sermons that deal with personal needs, or by dealing with biblical statements concerning spiritual growth, the church leader is often able to prevent problems that might otherwise arise. An understanding of psychology can greatly assist in this aspect of the church's ministry.

A familiarization with psychology contributes to a greater efficiency in the church's work

Following the resurrection, Jesus gave His disciples instructions concerning the future. The followers of Christ were commanded to preach, teach, and make disciples of the nations (Matthew 28:19-20; Mark 16:15). Psychological research findings concerning learning, communication, and persuasion are very relevant to the directives of the "great commission."

In addition to these, other areas of psychology can contribute to the church's work. Attitude formation and change, motivation, leadership, emotional reactions, and group interaction, for example, have been studied by psychology and are relevant to church work. The psychology of human adjustment can be useful as we prepare

21

missionaries to enter new cultures. Even the research methods of psychology are important. Psychologists have spent considerable time devising techniques that enable us to measure and carefully study human behavior. Many of these techniques can be useful in evaluating some of the work of the church.

A familiarization with psychology contributes to our ability to defend the faith

Many of the arguments that are used to attack the church and criticize Christianity are based on psychology. Assertions that "evangelism is really a form of mass hypnosis," "faith healing is just the influence of the power of suggestion," "Christianity is a crutch for the emotionally unstable," "demon activity is solely a creation of pre-scientific superstition," or "miracles are really misperceptions," are based on psychology and difficult for the churchman to answer if he does not have some understanding of psychological research and presuppositions.

These six reasons for the study of psychology might also serve as six goals for readers of this book. The topics to be discussed and the examples that are used in the following chapters are chosen in an attempt to assist the reader in understanding and applying psychology to the work of the church. As we pursue this task, however, we must keep psychology in its proper perspective.

Psychology in Perspective

Recently, a seminary professor presented the author with a challenging question. "If psychology is as important as you claim, why did God wait until the twentieth century to bring it into existence?"

It is rarely possible for man to know why God acts as He does. In a number of scriptural passages, God reveals His purposes in acting as He did at specific times in history.

We know, for example, why Christ came to earth (John 3:16, 10:10), why He died (I Peter 3:18), and why He returned to heaven after the resurrection (John 14:2,3). We know some of the attributes of God and we know a few reasons why men experience trials and tribulations. For the most part, however, God's ways and actions are beyond human understanding (Romans 11:33).

While acknowledging our real ignorance, we can nevertheless make some observations and speculations. Within recent years, God, in His sovereignty, has permitted man to make fantastic scientific and technological advances. The development of psychology is a part of this explosion of scientific knowledge. As man's understanding and control of the physical world develop, it is surely important that he develop an increased understanding and control of himself. At present, it appears that in spite of the rapid development in psychology, psychiatry, sociology, anthropology, and the other behavioral sciences, we still have a long way to go to catch up to the physical sciences. Before the present "knowledge explosion" in science, perhaps man did not need to know what modern psychology has discovered. All of this is a twentieth century "happening."

When Jesus gave His great commission to the church (Matthew 28:18-20), He told us *what* to do, but He said little about *how* to do it. The church, correctly we suggest, has made use of the findings of modern technology. We use modern organs and heating systems in our church buildings, we use radio and the printing press to spread the gospel message, we travel on church business in modern jets, and we are beginning to make use of the computer.[3] Perhaps psychology is another modern tool that can be used by church leaders.

Herein lies the crux of this whole chapter and perhaps the most important idea in the entire book. *Psychology is a valuable TOOL which church leaders, seeking the guidance of the Holy Spirit, can use in their Christian service. But we*

23

must never let psychology become THE WORK of the church.
Psychology can be useful in spreading the gospel, but
psychology is not the gospel. Psychological techniques
can be used to persuade men, but it is the Holy Spirit who
convicts men of sin. Psychology can be a valuable tool in
Christian teaching, counseling, and self-understanding, but
it is God in the person of the Holy Spirit who teaches,
comforts, instructs, and guides.

One of the regretful developments in the pastoral psychology movement has been the over-emphasis on
psychology with a corresponding decline in the influence
of the Scripture. Pastors sometimes have become so
impressed with psychology that they have become full-time
counselors who use psychological techniques almost exclusively and have little time left for prayer, study, and
careful sermon preparation. Bible study and prayer groups
have become group therapy sessions. Seminary faculties
have reduced the number of required theology and Bible
courses and replaced these with an over-abundance of
psychology, sociology, and counseling courses. Such an
over-aceptance of psychology adulterates the distinctive
character of churches and emasculates the Christian gospel.

Psychology is an exciting and potentially practical modern
development. When church leaders use it carefully and with
a desire to be led of God, psychology can have a great
positive influence in the work of the church. But we must
be careful to insure that psychology is kept in perspective
—as a useful tool.

Normal Human Development

Many centuries ago, the wisest of Israel's kings gave some
advice that could well apply to parents and Sunday school
teachers today. "Train up a child in the way he should go,"

24

wrote King Solomon, "and when he is old, he will not depart from it" (Proverbs 22:6). Many years later, the apostle Paul wrote in a similar vein. "Children, obey your parents for this is right. . . . And now a word to you parents. Don't keep on scolding and nagging your children, making them angry and resentful. But bring them up with the loving discipline the Lord Himself approves, with suggestions and godly advice" (Ephesians 6:1,4, Living Letters).

These writers believed that the upbringing of children had an important bearing on their future character and behavior. Plato would have agreed. So would John Locke and hundreds of other writers from the beginning of history down to this age of Benjamin Spock and Haim Ginott.

When the scientific study of human development began, less than a century ago, the focus of attention was almost exclusively on children and adolescents. Later, developmental psychologists began to extend their study to include adulthood and old age. Today, although most research still centers on the first twenty years of life (during this period the most significant changes occur), it is widely recognized that development begins at the instant of conception and continues until the moment of death.

There are at least three reasons why church workers should know something about normal human development. First, such knowledge enables us to better understand individual people. Why does an occasional six-year-old become the terror of a Sunday school or how do you explain the gigling of thirteen-year-old girls? A familiarization with child development and adolescent psychology can help us to answer such questions. Why do middle-aged people get depressed or older people become rigid in their thinking? The actions of a man "when he is old" are determined to some extent by his training as a child, but living through middle and old age involves some typical frustrations and pressures. When we know about these we can better understand the problems and behavior of people in the second-half of life. Secondly, our understanding of social problems is increased when we know how prejudice, hostility, or other social attitudes begin in childhood and then become part of the adult personality. Thirdly, an understanding of human development makes our practical ministry more relevant and helpful. When we know how little children learn, how students adjust to college, or how older people react to forced retirement, for example, Christian education programs and counseling activities can be altered and made more effective. Even in evangelism, if we are familiar with the thinking and outlook of children, teenagers, college students and other age groups, we can know better how to approach these different people with the Gospel.

The characteristics and problems of one age group may differ significantly from those of another age group. For this reason, we will deal in separate chapters with childhood, adolescence, young adulthood, and the middle and older years. In spite of the age differences, however, there are some principles of development that apply to the young and old alike. As we consider normal human development, especially in children, it is wise to keep the following four principles in mind.

DEVELOPMENT IS ORDERLY AND IN SEQUENCES

There are exceptions, of course, but usually people develop through specific stages—one leading to the next. A child stands before he walks, crawls before he talks, draws circles before squares, runs with a gang before he starts "going steady." Development usually proceeds from general responses to specific actions. The baby waves his whole arm long before he can make the precise wrist and finger movements required to pick up a small object. He talks of "doggies" before he can differentiate between a poodle and a pekingese (Hurlock, 1964).

DEVELOPMENT IS UNEVEN

Every parent is familiar with "growth spurts." During the first couple of years the child grows rapidly. Following this, development becomes more gradual and then with the onset of adolescence, another growth spurt occurs. Most human development takes place in this irregular fashion. The central nervous system develops very early in life and then growth slows down. The reproductive organs do not develop much until adolescence, but then they mature rapidly. The use of vocabulary seems to blossom suddenly during preschool years, and parents are often surprised to see their teenagers quickly change in social maturity after a long and immature adolescence. In one of the earliest studies of learning, Bryan and Harter (1897) discovered that to acquire some skills, we start with a period of rapid improvement and then level off—sometimes for weeks—before we begin to show improvement again.

DEVELOPMENT IS UNIQUE

While everyone passes through stages, no two people develop at exactly the same rate. A mother may gloat because her two-year-old has a larger vocabulary than the neighbor's child, but the child next door may suddenly overtake and surpass every other two-year-old in the neighborhood. After a lifetime studying the behavior of young children, Dr. Arnold Gesell, concluded that "no two children are exactly alike...no two...grow up in just the same way. Every child has a distinctive style or method of growth" (Gesell & Ilg, 1949, p. 43). In intellectual, physical, social, and emotional development, people mature at different rates and in unique ways. This applies at all age levels.

DEVELOPMENT IS THE RESULT OF BOTH MATURATION AND LEARNING

Maturation refers to the changes that take place automatically within a biological organism. These physical changes are not dependent on environmental influences. In contrast, learning can be thought of as a change in behavior or performance which comes about as as a result of experience. It is difficult to distinguish between developmental changes that result from learning and those which arise from maturation, but both are of great importance. This point is one that few if any psychologists would dispute.

In the following pages we will consider how these four principles of development apply to different age groups. The typical characteristics of children, adolescents, and adults will be summarized; the spiritual development at different ages will be discussed; and an attempt will be made to understand some of the problems and obstacles that must be overcome as people pass through the various stages of life. All of these topics will be related to the concerns and work of the church leader.

As we grow older, we all encounter stresses which make life more difficult—and challenging. In the last chapter of this section we will consider the nature of stress and the ways in which normal people respond to the difficulties of life.

Summary

Modern psychology, which began in the latter part of the 19th century, can be defined as a science and an art which studies the directly observable behavior of men and animals and the less directly observable feelings, thoughts, motives, and self-concepts that cause or accompany such behavior. Psychologists work in a variety of settings and perform a number of important tasks. In spite of the growth of this field, however, there are still a number of popular misconceptions about the nature and work of psychologists.

The application of psychology to the work of the church is a relatively recent development. It began with the interest of forward-thinking churchmen who persisted in their efforts in spite of psychology's general lack of interest in religion. At present, pastoral psychology has grown to become a significant movement which examines psychological research and insights, evaluates these from a theological and biblical perspective, and attempts to determine how these can apply to the work of pastors and other church leaders.

For several reasons, contemporary church leaders can benefit from a careful study of modern psychology. We must remember, however, that psychology is a tool of the church worker. It must never become *the* main work of the church but should be used instead while the Christian leader seeks to be guided by the Holy Spirit.

Regardless of his place of service, the church leader will be dealing with normal people. To understand how people develop and how they face and overcome their problems is to increase one's effectiveness in working with others. To increase this understanding is the goal of the chapters which follow

Chapter Two

CHILDHOOD: THE FORMATIVE YEARS

During His earthly ministry, Jesus showed a sincere concern for little children. One example of this is seen in an event that is described in three of the four gospels. Apparently it was a busy day! The crowds were great and the Lord was involved in preaching, answering questions and healing the sick. In the midst of this activity some parents tried to push through the crowd and bring their children to Jesus in order that he might "put his hands on them and pray" (Matthew 19:13). The disciples, who probably wanted to protect Jesus from unnecessary distractions, turned the parents back. In the opinion of the twelve, there were more important things for the Lord to do, but Jesus saw what was happening and intervened. "Let the children come to me," he said, "do not hinder them" (Luke 18:16, RSV). Then he took them in his arms, put his hands upon them, and blessed them (Mark 10:16).

On another occasion the disciples asked who would be greatest in the kingdom of heaven. They must have been surprised when Jesus called a child, set him in their midst and announced that "it is the man who can be as humble as this little child who is greatest in the kingdom of Heaven." Then Jesus talked about the way in which children should be treated. "Anyone who welcomes one child like this for my sake is welcoming me. But if anyone leads astray one of these little children who believe in me he would be better off thrown into the depths of the sea with a mill-stone hung round his neck! (Matthew 18:4-6, Phillips).

31

Church members, whether or not they are parents, have a divinely given example and responsibility to guide in the up-bringing of children. But how is this to be done? The Bible gives only a few general principles. Psychologists and child guidance experts may give advice but this is sometimes confusing and even contradictory. Parents do their best but often feel frustrated and perplexed as they strive to raise children "in the discipline and instruction of the Lord" (Eph. 6:4, RSV).

While there is disagreement over the proper ways of raising and educating children, there is considerable agreement concerning childhood characteristics. Developmental psychologists have conducted literally thousands of studies and the results of these investigations have substantially increased our knowledge and understanding of the nature of childhood. A survey of some of these psychological conclusions could be of value to church leaders and Christian parents as they seek to "train up a child in the way he should go" (Proverbs 22:6). Let us start with the beginning of life —nine months prior to the child's birth.

The Prenatal Period

At the time of sexual intercourse, millions of tiny sperm cells are thrust into the channels of the female reproductive system. If one of these sperm cells from the father comes into contact with the egg (ovum) from the mother, the egg is fertilized and a new life has been started. This one fertilized cell, which is only 1/175 inch in diameter, soon divides into two cells, then into 4, then 8, 16, 32, and so on. After about 226 days (which is the average length of a pregnancy) an intricately formed child, composed of billions of cells, is born.

As with physical development, the process of psychological maturation begins long before birth. Studies have demonstrated that much of an individual's subsequent personality and behavior is determined at the moment of conception and during those nine months when the child is developing in his mother's womb.

The Influence of Heredity

When the sperm penetrates the wall of the ovum, twenty-three tiny particles, known as *chromosomes,* are released. At about the same time, the inner core of the egg cell breaks up and releases another twenty-three chromosomes. These forty-six chromosomes—twenty-three from each parent —are composed of smaller particles called *genes.* The genes are very important because they are carriers of the child's heredity. One of the reasons for individual differences is that each of us receives a unique combination of genes. Even children from the same parents are not likely to inherit similar genes (except when there are identical twins), and therefore obvious individual differences exist within the same family.

What does the child inherit at the time of conception? Research is still being conducted in an attempt to answer this question, but some things are certain. Physical characteristics such as sex, eye color, facial features, skin pigment, color and curliness of hair, and general body build pretty much result from heredity. Some forms of mental retardation are also inherited. But what about intelligence, personality characteristics, mental disorders, or susceptibility to disease?

It is difficult to know what comes from heredity and what results from environmental influences. We know, for example, that if one twin develops a mental illness, the other is likely to do so also. But twins are similar in more than their heredity. They have the same parents, usually live in the same house, and experience many of the same pressures. It may be, then, that mental disorders result from similarities in environment instead of, or in addition to, similarities in heredity. To a large extent, therefore, the evidence is still inconclusive concerning the exact influence that heredity plays in determining human behavior.

We can know for certain, however, that heredity and environmental influences work together to mold a lot of behavior. Because of their inheritance, some people are more inclined to be fat, or socially outgoing, or "good looking," or intellectually brilliant, or susceptible to heart attacks. But whether these, and a host of other characteristics will materialize, and the extent to which they will materialize, depends on the experiences that people have as they pass through life.

Prenatal Environmental Influences

It was once thought that the environment didn't have any influence until the time of birth, but now we know that life experiences begin shortly after the time of conception. Even before he is born, the individual's physical and emotional future may be influenced by the experiences, health, and attitudes of the mother.

Consider, for example, the influences of *disease.* The unborn child (which, for most of the pregnancy, is called a fetus) is so well protected that it is rare for a mother's illness to be transmitted or for fetal development to be hindered because of maternal sickness. It is well known, however, that German measles is a disease which *can* influence the unborn child, causing deaf-mutism, visual deformities, heart problems, or mental deficiency. Usually, measles is damaging only if contracted within the first three months of pregnancy, and even then in eighty-eight per cent of the cases there is no detectable harm to the fetus (Greenberg, Pelliteri, and Barton, 1957).

The *mother's physical makeup* can also be important. Women who are under twenty or over thirty-five years of age, and those whose blood type is chemically incompatable with that of the fetus, have a higher incidence of retarded or deformed babies. Also, inadequate *diet,* large doses of *x-ray* radiation, and the taking of certain *drugs* can be harmful. Early in the 1960's a drug known as thalidomide appeared on the market in Europe and was widely used for relief of coughs, colds, headaches, and the symptoms of nausea and morning sickness. Only after the birth of several thousand deformed babies was it discovered that thalidomide, along with its medicinal value, was also hindering the normal development of limbs and other organs in unborn infants (Taussig, 1962). [1]

Perhaps of greatest interest to church workers is the influence on the fetus of the mother's *emotional state and attitudes* during pregnancy. Short periods of emotional stress may stimulate the fetus to move more frequently, but this is temporary and harmless. More influencial is the presence of extreme anxiety, tension, and prolonged emotional turmoil during pregnancy. This can lead to delivery complications and the birth of emotionally distressed babies. Even the mother's attitude is important. In one study, those women who had unfavorable attitudes toward their pregnancy later had babies with eating problems, many bowel movements, frequent gas pains, inability to sleep at night, large amounts of crying, and unusual needs to be held (Mussen, Conger, and Kagan, 1969; Davids, DeVault and Talmadge, 1961). [2] One author has described these infants.

> He is to all intents and purposes a neurotic infant when he is born—the result of an unsatisfactory fetal environment. In this instance, he has not had to wait until childhood for a bad home situation or other cause to make him neurotic. It has been done for him before he has even seen the light of day (Sontag, 1944).

Prenatal Religious Development
There is debate among theologians concerning the possibility and extent of spiritual development prior to birth.

In a provocative article published in *Christianity Today,* one seminary professor argued that faith is possible even prior to birth. He cites the leaping of the baby in Elizabeth's womb (Luke 1:44) in support of his conclusions (Scaer, 1967).

Whatever one's theological response to this suggestion, there is no psychological evidence to support the idea that a fetus (or very young child) can "have sufficient consciousness or mental development to make coming to faith possible." We know that learning can occur in unborn infants after the sixth month of pregnancy, but the only learning of which they are capable is to make simple physical responses to conditioned stimulations. There is as yet no evidence to support the idea that more complicated thinking or learning is possible (Spelt, 1948).

The leaping of the unborn John the Baptist in his mother's womb may have resulted from factors other than "belief" by the fetus. In Luke 1:41 we read that Elizabeth *heard* Mary's voice before the child leaped. It has already been mentioned that the fetus will often move following an experience of strong emotion in the mother. It is highly probable that Elizabeth experienced such emotion when she heard Mary's voice. For an individual to have faith in Christ, he must be able to discriminate between alternatives (to believe or not to believe), think abstractly (belief in Christ is not very tangible), understand language, be able to use language (Romans 10:9a), and be able to perceive time (to realize the future implications of his present decision). There is no scientific evidence to suggest that any of these exists in unborn or very young children. Apparently prior to their birth some people are set apart by God for special service (Jer. 1:5; Luke 1:13-17; Eph. 1:4, 5) but there is no psychological evidence and apparently no biblical evidence to support the idea that spiritual development occurs in the unborn.

36

Implications For Church Leaders

Even though the fetus is incapable of belief, the church can make at least three contributions to the welfare of the unborn child. First, the church leader can encourage the pregnant mother to get prenatal medical care if she is not doing so already. Most of the harmful prenatal environmental influences which we have listed are of a physical nature and almost all can be reduced or eliminated with proper medical attention.

Secondly, the pastoral counselor can help the prospective parents to accept their feelings about the pregnancy. It is not unusual for expectant parents to have periods of doubt and disappointment, especially during first and unplanned pregnancies. The birth of a child can put financial and emotional strain on a marriage and sometimes there is considerable readjustment and inconvenience. At times both parents may decide that they don't want the child, and these feelings are usually followed by guilt. When he encourages parents to talk about their feelings, points out that such attitudes are common, and helps parents to make realistic plans, the church leader is contributing much to the reduction of prenatal parental tension and anxiety. Parents can also be encouraged to attend the special evening classes that are offered for pregnant women and their husbands at most large hospitals. These classes give helpful information about pregnancy and childbirth and this in turn often reduces anxiety.

Thirdly, the parents can be encouraged and guided in the establishing of a Christian home. When parents seek to make Christ central in the home, tensions are reduced (this is good for the fetus) and the stage is set for the spiritual growth of the child after birth. Even prior to pregnancy, parents should learn to pray together, to read the Bible, and to seek the leading of the Holy Spirit in decision making.

The birth of a child occurs in three stages. In stage one, which is the longest, the opening of the womb (cervix) slowly enlarges to permit passage of the baby's head. In stage two, the baby passes through the vagina and eventually is delivered to the outside world. In the third stage the *afterbirth* or placenta is delivered. This is the tissue which nourished and protected the fetus prior to birth. When the delivery is completed, the physician usually gives the mother a hormone injection which hastens the shrinking of the uterus and presses shut any broken bleeding blood vessels.

Although the mother may think otherwise, the newborn baby is not very beautiful. Often reddish blue, wrinkled and covered with a waxy oil-covering, his head may be out of shape and his body is likely to appear scrawny.

In spite of this uninspiring appearance, the newborn child is a remarkably capable organism from the moment he begins to breathe. He can see, hear, and smell, and is sensitive to (some) pain, touch, and change in position. The only one of the five senses that may not be functioning immediately at birth is taste.

The newborn's behavioral equipment is also remarkably well-developed. When only two hours old, he will follow a rapidly moving light with his eyes; his pupils will dilate in darkness and constrict in light; he will suck a finger or nipple inserted in his mouth; he will turn in the direction in which his cheek or the corner of his mouth is touched. He can cry, cough, turn away, vomit, lift his chin from a prone position, and grasp an object placed in his palm. His body will react to a loud sound. He can flex and extend his limbs, smack his lips, and chew his fingers.

It is fortunate that the infant is so competent at birth because his new environment outside his mother's body subjects him suddenly to such unfamiliar stresses as hunger, heat, cold, and pain (Kagan, 1968, p. 80).

The subsequent development of this little creature during his first year of life is difficult to summarize concisely. Several thousand studies have focused on this period of life and a tremendous volume of information is available. These studies have shown that change is rapid and that young children differ considerably from one another in spite of the similarities that do exist among infants.

Characteristics of Infancy

Development during the first year of life is characterized by rapid physical growth, initial perceptual and intellectual development, a learning to cope with new experiences, early social and emotional development, and the beginnings of personality formation.

The details of the infant's *physical growth* have been carefully described by Gessell and his colleagues (1940, 1943, 1949, 1952; Ilg and Ames, 1955). For our purposes, therefore, it is sufficient to mention only the major changes that occur during the first twelve months. In this period the infant triples his birth weight and his length increases over one-third. By his first birthday, the typical child has six teeth, is able to sit without support, can crawl (and often walk), picks up small objects between his thumb and finger, follows moving objects with his eyes, and vocalizes a few words. This development is a drastic change from the helpless newborn who could not even hold up his head. These physical changes are the result of maturation—the physical growth which occurs independent of learning or experience. Impatient parents can try to hasten a child's sitting or walking, but such early physical changes occur when the muscles and nerves have sufficiently developed —and not before.

Perceptual and intellectual development are interdependent. Most psychologists no longer agree with William James (1890) that the newborn experiences a "blooming, buzzing confusion" of stimulations. Observations suggest that rather than being overwhelmed with sights and sounds, little children instead experience a vaguely perceptible background of meaningless sensations. Slowly, as he grows older, the infant learns to recognize objects and people, to become aware of the meaning of stimulations, and to discover that there is a part of the world which is "me"— distinctly separate from the rest of the environment. In short, much of life during the first year involves learning to make sense of the world.

Making sense of the world is difficult when one does not understand language. A Swiss psychologist named Jean Piaget carefully studied perceptual and intellectual development during the first year and concluded that development in this period occurs in four stages. In the first stage (which lasts for about a month) the child learns through his reflexes. Repetition of sucking, blinking, crying, and rhythm in breathing teach him how to adapt to some of the stimulations in his environment. In the second stage (second month) the child learns that he has voluntary control over some of the responses which were previously automatic. He can suck, stare, make noises, and move his thumb to his mouth—all by himself. The third stage lasts about six months (third to ninth month). During this time the child learns that events can persist for a period of time and thus he wants repeated and prolonged experience with stimuli. An object such as a toy, for example, is looked at, sucked, tugged, waved, rubbed against the floor, dropped. It is at this stage that the child first begins to imitate, play, and show emotion. The fourth stage which occurs at the end of the first year, is characterized by random experimentation. The child is now able to get around a little and he experiences everything available. He learns that objects continue to exist even if they are hidden, and he learns the meaning of a few words like "bye-bye" or "go outside" (Piaget, 1963; Maier, 1965). For all of this to occur, of course, the child must be in an environment which provides much varied stimulation.

Coping with new experiences begins in infancy, but continues through life. The little child soon discovers that society has certain ways of doing things. His family, for example, has certain routines and believes that the sooner the child learns to adjust to these, the better. In a book on coping behavior, Dr. Lois Murphy (1962) concluded that infants must learn to adapt to six major tasks: managing body functions like feedings, sleeping, elimination, etc.; dealing with environmental stimulation; adapting to changes in routine and abilities—such as weaning; mastering illness and other traumas; learning to move about in the environment; and acquiring the social expectations of his family situation. Apparently little children are plastic enough that they can make these adaptations quickly (Campbell, 1968).

However, individual differences in children's coping behavior vary greatly. According to one psychologist, "infants differ widely in their capacity to tolerate coercion, deprivation, and frustration, some reacting vigorously while others may passively accept such treatment and exhibit no overt reactions" (Frank, 1966, pp. 116-117). The writer goes on to say that because they are helpless and dependent, infants pick up and reflect the emotional climate of the home. When there is tension, marital discord or even excessive commotion in a home, babies respond with crying. Conversely, a disturbed infant may settle down immediately in the arms of a stranger after a frustrated mother has tried for a long time without success to calm her child. Apparently, the infant perceives and feels composure in the stranger's calmness.

The *social and emotional development* which occurs in infancy is primarily the result of learning. (It is a major theme of this book that most behavior is learned.) The infant, from the beginning of life, experiences contact with other people. At first he experiences a communion or emotional bond with the mother which has been called *empathy* (Sullivan, 1940). Later he begins to recognize the father and others, but he may show fear in the presence of strangers. By the time he is one, the baby is still primarily self-centered but he heeds and seeks the stimulation that comes from contact with others.

It is difficult to know what emotions are experienced by infants. Since we can't ask the baby what he is feeling, we must guess on the basis of our observations of his behavior. Our guesses, of course, may very well be wrong since the baby has not learned how to express emotion like we do in our society. Many years ago, one study suggested that during the first year, children experience excitement, distress, delight, anger, disgust, fear, elation, and affection (Bridges, 1932). Others have compiled different lists. At present, therefore, it seems wise to conclude only that young children are capable of some feelings and that they learn how to express their emotions as they grow older.

Personality development, like the experience of emotion, begins early in life. After a careful study of the research on infancy, Frank concluded that "each child, beginning in infancy, develops his own 'life style,' his idiomatic patterns of functioning, activity and responsiveness to the demands and opportunities of living" (1966, p. 129). Of course, personality is being molded throughout life and behavior can change, but experiences during the early months seem to largely influence one's later personality characteristics and outlook on life.

Consider, for example, the development of trust. Early in life, the child learns either that the world is a good and satisfying place to live, or that it is a source of pain, frustration, fear, and uncertainty. He develops either a basic trust or a basic mistrust. If he develops a basic mistrust, according to Erickson (1963), his subsequent personality development will be hindered, and colored by his attitude.

Religious Development

Psychologists have had very little to say about spiritual development in infancy. Religious beliefs and concepts are meaningless to the young child and he is not old enough to appreciate the rituals and solemnity of church services.

Indirectly, however, religion does have an influence on the infant. Children live in and must adapt to a home setting. In this environment the parents' religion, or lack of it, has a considerable effect. One study showed, for example, that religious beliefs influence not only the parents' habits of worship, but also their attitudes toward work, installment buying, and savings; their political behavior and preferences; their family relationships and opinions about childrearing; and their view of sin (Lenski, 1961). Although the infant understands none of this, he can detect and react to this home atmosphere which is created in part by parental religious beliefs. The infant responds not to what the parents say they believe but to their behavior and attitudes.

Potential Problems

The problems that will be encountered in infancy will depend somewhat on the culture. In English-speaking North America, problems usually center around feeding, weaning, sleeping, thumb-sucking, excessive crying and, later, toilet training. In years gone by, the mother gained support, encouragement and advice on these matters from experienced and sympathetic relatives but this has all changed with the current mobility of families (in the United States approximately one family in every four moves each year). Relatives are now often far away, and the young parents who reside in relatively unfamiliar communities must depend more on books and articles—some of which give conflicting and confusing advice.

43

Regardless of the culture, one issue always has a direct bearing on infant well-being. This is the importance of stimulation and maternal love. Abundant evidence has accumulated which shows that physical and psychological damage can come to the infant who does not have close contact with an adult. The extent and quality of the damage varies with the age at which deprivation occurs, the length of time during which it exists, and the quality of substitute care that is provided (Bowlby, 1952). Apparently, vulnerability is maximum during early infancy (three-six months). During World War II, Spitz (1945) studied children who were raised in institutions where the physical care was adequate but the stimulation was minimal. When compared with children in normal families, the institutionalized children were slow in learning to walk and talk, unhealthy, listless, unresponsive to adults, poor eaters, and generally unhappy. It appears that frequent stimulation and plenty of "tender loving care" are absolute necessities for the healthy development of a child (Ambrose, 1970).

Table 2-1 summarizes unhealthy home situations which can adversely influence the child. While the very young child can develop problems because of these undesirable home situations, the older child is even more likely to be affected.

Implications for Church Leaders

Perhaps at no time is the Christian church worker less able to make a direct impact on a life than in infancy. The infant cannot understand religious concepts, and most of his learning—religious and otherwise—occurs in the home. The church's impact, therefore, must be indirect. It is by working with the family that we can most effectively minister to the developing child.

Since the home atmosphere is so important in infant development, the church leader must encourage good interpersonal relations between family members. This can be

Table 2—1

Faulty Parent-Child Relationships *

Undesirable Condition	Typical Influence on Child
Rejection	Feelings of insecurity and isolation. Attention-seeking, negativistic hostile behavior. Unable to give and receive affection.
Overprotection—domination	Submission, inadequacy, lack of initiative, tendency to passive dependency in relations with others.
Overindulgence	Selfish, demanding, with inability to tolerate frustration. Rebellious to authority, excessive need of attention, lack of responsibility.
Perfectionism—unrealistic ambitions for child	Child internalizes parents' unrealistic standards. Inevitable failure leads to continual frustration, guilt, and self-devaluation.
Rigid, unrealistic moral standards	Extreme conscience development. Tendency to rigidity, severe conflicts, guilt, self-condemnation, and self-devaluation.
Faulty discipline	Overpermissiveness often leads to insecurity, antisocial aggressiveness. Severe discipline typically results in excessive condemnation of self for socially disapproved behavior and anxiety over aggressive actions. Inconsistent discipline commonly results in a lack of stable values for guiding behavior along with a tendency to inconsistency and vacillation in meeting problems.
Sibling rivalry	Direct or indirect hostility, insecurity, lack of self-confidence, regression.
Marital discord and broken homes	Anxiety, tension, insecurity, lack of secure home base, a tendency to evaluate the world as a dangerous and insecure place. Conflicting loyalties and a lack of adequate models for proper development.
Faulty parental models	Internalization of unethical and socially undesirable value attitudes that frequently lead to difficulties with the law.
Contradictory demands	Lack of integrated frame of reference; confusion and self-devaluation.

The exact effects of faulty parent-child relationships on later behavior depend on many factors, including the age of the child, the constitutional and personality make-up of the child, the duration and degree of the unhealthy relationship, the child's perception of the relationship, and the total family setting and life context, including the presence or absence of alleviating conditions and whether or not subsequent experiences tend to reinforce or correct early damage.

* Adapted from "Summary Chart of Faulty Parent-Child Relationships." From *Abnormal Psychology and Modern Life*, Third Edition by James C. Coleman. Copyright 1964 by Scott, Foresman and Company. *(used by permission)*

done through sermons on the Christian home, casual discussions with the parents, personal counseling, or periodic reference to practical books such as those listed at the end of this book under *Suggestions for Further Reading.*

Most churches have some ceremony of dedication or sprinkling for infants. The author can find no scriptural basis to suggest that such acts bestow salvation, but the ceremony can have real significance for the parents and the church members. When Jesus was presented in the temple, His parents were reminded of their spiritual obligations, and they were encouraged by the words of devoted servants of God (Luke 2:21-38). In like manner the service of dedication can be a reminder to the parents of their responsibilities before God, and a charge to the congregation to pray for and encourage those who have the joyful task of raising little children. Some churches enter the child's name on a "cradle roll" in anticipation of future Sunday school training, and cradle roll workers then visit the parents and send descriptive literature during the child's first year or two of life.

The Preschool Years

According to Freud, the first five years of life are decisive in the formation of personality. While it may be that Freud overemphasized the importance of early life, it is certain that a number of radically significant changes do occur during the years between a child's first birthday and the time he enters school about four years later.

Characteristics of Preschoolers

By the time he is five, the average child is about three and one-half feet tall and weighs forty-three pounds. His muscles have developed to the extent that he has mastered such diverse skills as riding a tricycle, galloping, skipping, or dancing tip-toe to music. In addition to physical and motor development, the preschooler shows important progress in other areas. Chief of these are (1) thinking, intelligence and language use, (2) social development, (3) personality growth, and (4) emotional behavior. Each of these issues will be discussed briefly along with the child's play activities and his increasing awareness of sex.

When a child learns a *language,* his *thinking, intelligence,* perceiving and feeling is transformed.

> ...by understanding speech...the child becomes open to endless verbal instruction, he can learn...through the words of others, he can enter realms of knowledge, such as history, that he can never know firsthand, he can dwell in the virtual realms created by writers of stories and poetry, and he can learn accessory means of expression and manipulation like drawing and arithmetic. On the side of coming to speak, the child can convey his thoughts and feelings and wishes to others, he can think and reason and make sense of and order his own experience, he can make original statements, and he can concoct fantasies, jokes and works of imagination (Stone & Church, 1968, p. 231).

It might also be added that with language comes the ability to learn about God and the lives of Bible characters.

The young child probably understands much more than he can say. As adults talk he hears their words, but at the same time he gets information from adult gestures, tones of voice, and facial expressions. He also sees the context in which the statement was made. "You spilled your milk," for example, is a statement that is likely to be accompanied by adult activity and the experience of a white liquid flowing all over the table or into the child's lap.

Sometime near the beginning of the second year, the child reaches the first step in language—he says single words, largely in the form of requests or descriptive statements

47

("bed" may mean "I want to go to bed," or "there's my bed"). The second step is "expressive jargon." The child jabbers with a lot of gibberish which is probably intended to convey meaning but which is nonsense to anyone other than the child. The third stage involves the putting together of two, and then more words. Later, the sentences lengthen and the grammar becomes more correct. By the third birthday, most children are talking fluently—although in simple fashion. Shortly thereafter they begin to ask "why"—often just to keep the conversation going.

Children learn language in a casual way. Initially, their speech is imitation; later they compose their own phrases. In either case, when the child says something that is meaningful or grammatically correct, the parents usually respond with recognition and sometimes praise. If this happens the word or phrase stays in the vocabulary and is sometimes repeated several times. If the child says something which is meaningless or incorrect, and there is no parental praise, the phrase drops out. Obviously when a child has no adult or older companions his language development is slowed down.

Even when there are ample opportunities to talk language development does not progress with perfect understanding. Church workers are surprised to discover that children talk of "Jesus and the twelve bicycles" (disciples) or sing such things as "Lead on O Twiggy turtle" (King Eternal) or "the grandpas we watched were so gallantly screaming" (the ramparts we watched, were so gallantly streaming). It has also been observed that a child's language is often accompanied by actions. The young child acts out his thoughts so that thinking and speaking are simultaneous. Piaget calls this "thinking aloud." During the preschool years, children also assume that everyone thinks alike and that almost all events center around the thinker (e.g. "night comes because I'm tired").

Children's thinking most often proceeds from the concrete to the abstract. The child, for example, can understand "dog" before he comprehends the meaning of "animal." When asked to indicate in what way an orange and banana are alike, the very young child says "they both have skins" (concrete and tangible), the older child says "you can eat them" (concrete and functional) and only later can the child give an abstract reply like "they're both fruit." Such knowledge has practical implications for those who teach little children in Sunday school. Stories about Jesus and little children are much more meaningful than stories about "love" or "giving." It should be noted, however, that the progression from concrete to abstract does not always hold. With some terms, the abstract is learned first (Brown, 1958). [3]

In addition to learning a language, the preschooler is also very much involved in *social development*. If he is to get along as an adult, he must learn and accept the behavior, values, and attitudes which are characteristic of his society. This social learning begins in the home and usually starts as a result of "identification." This term refers to a person's learning to think, feel and behave as though the characteristics of another belong to him. The child recognizes that adults have power, privileges, and skills which children do not possess. If, in addition, the parents are warm and loving, the child seeks to possess all of the adult characteristics. To do so he imitates the parents and tries to model his behavior after theirs. If, as often happens, adults compliment the child for these "grown-up" actions, he is encouraged to repeat the imitations and eventually he comes to be like the parents. As the child grows older, he identifies with the behavior of teachers, other adults, peers, and (when he gets into his teens) adolescent heros (Mussen, Conger, & Kagan, 1969; Hoppe, Milton, & Simmel, 1970).

At the same time, he is learning to get along with other children. The very young preschooler may simply regard other young people as curiosities. At two, children do a lot of pushing and hitting but around age three they are able to play in a parallel fashion—in the same location, but often with no real interaction. Next, children enjoy playing in little groups. They run, climb, giggle or act foolish together. Sometimes they even "converse" although this may involve two children talking in alternate succession about two completely different and unrelated topics. During this age, children in our culture often develop sympathy for others, aggression, competition, jealousy and leadership abilities. At three or four they sometimes select a special friend, but these friends are changed frequently (Stone & Church, 1968). In summary, the preschooler is learning to be less self-centered, to appreciate the feelings and opinions of others, and to act in a socially appropriate fashion. This is a process which continues for many years and is greatly influenced by the frequency and nature of contact with other children. Most psychologists believe that nursery school speeds up the preschooler's progress and greatly aids social development (Hattwick, 1936; Mussen, Conger, & Kagan, 1969).

Perhaps this would be a good point for a consideration of children's *play*. While adults may tend to consider this to be useless activity, play serves at least four important functions. First, play permits the discharge of energy in little bodies that need to engage in vigorous activity. Second, play provides stimulation. Without new and varied experiences, all of us—including children—would be unhappy, bored, and retarded in our development (Fiske & Maddi, 1961). Third, play enables the child to develop his motor skills. Pounding pegs, pulling a wagon, digging in a sandbox, riding a tricycle and (much later) playing basketball, all develop muscular coordination and perfection of physical skills (Radler, 1960). Fourth, play teaches the child about adult roles. When he "plays house" or "plays school," the child is experiencing and practicing adult behavior. Such play is also a reflection of how the child views

50

the world. Often his fears, hostilities, and expectations are reflected in his reenactment of adult roles.

As with other aspects of development, forms of play show a progression. The infant enjoys "social-affective" play in which he is tickled, snuggled or otherwise stimulated by adults. Later, the child enjoys "sense-pleasure" play in which he can experience water, mud, singing, jumping and other sensory experiences. "Skill" play involves such activities as piling blocks, running, or riding a tricycle, and then comes "dramatic" play in which the child acts out adult roles. This is followed by "formal games." Sometimes these are simple, like London Bridge; later they are more complicated. All of these kinds of play can be done in the company of others, and nearly all are present, not only in the preschool years, but on into adulthood (Stone & Church, 1968).

Of additional importance in the study of children is an understanding of their *personality growth* and development. This topic has interested psychologists for many years. Freud, for example, developed an elaborate personality theory based on sexual drives. Erikson (1963) concluded that personality develops throughout life, and stressed that the preschooler must learn to be autonomous and to develop a sense of initiative. Other theorists have reached different conclusions—some based on research and some based on speculation (Hall & Lindzey, 1970; Smith, 1968; Walters & Bandura, 1963). While all of this psychological theorizing is important, it is enough for our understanding of preschoolers to say that personality is greatly influenced by the events of his early life. His physical build, inherited characteristics, temperament, rate of maturing and other biological features have a bearing on the way in which he reacts to the world and on the ways in which others, in turn, react to him. The expectations of the culture influence one's personality and, of even greater significance are the effects of personal experiences with family, friends, and other individuals.

51

Emotions also play an important part in the preschooler's life. As he learns to interact with his environment he experiences many feelings that he expresses freely. Most often seen are fears (especially at around three years), anxiety, anger (temper tantrums are frequent between two and four years), jealousy (especially if a new baby is born when the child is between two and five years), curiosity, joy, delight, and affection (Hurlock, 1964). When they are frustrated, preschool children sometimes withdraw from the situation, sometimes blame others for their troubles, and sometimes regress to baby-like behavior (such as a four-year-old who, frustrated over the arrival of a new baby sister, begins wetting his pants again). Later, frustration may bring anger or aggression and with older children there may be more constructive attempts to overcome problems (Mussen, Conger, & Kagan, 1969). Regardless of what causes the feelings, children's emotions are typically brief in duration, intense, frequent in occurence, and often brought on by what adults consider to be matters of minor importance. Children differ considerably in their emotional expression and as they grow older; emotions change in strength—some become stronger, some weaker (Hurlock, 1964). Apparently emotion, like most other of the preschoolers' characteristics, is greatly influenced by learning.

Children also learn something about *sex*. Freud (1938) believed that sex was basic to the development of young children, and his famous theory described in detail the supposed sexual urges and behavior of the first six years of life. While few psychologists accept Freud's theories today, it is generally agreed that preschoolers are curious about male-female differences. They are very interested in anatomy and whenever possible they carefully observe the bodies of parents and peers—especially those of the opposite sex. Children are uninhibited in their talk and questions about the body and often they will engage in open masturbation. The ways in which parents react to this sexual curiosity are very important. When parents honestly answer the questions at the child's level of understanding and calmly point out that some things are always talked about privately, the child's attitudes toward sex are much healthier than those of children whose parents condemn the curiosity and give evidence of being embarassed. The child recognizes that this must be some especially important topic and he may wonder what all of the fuss is about. In any case, by the time they start school, children are well aware that boys and girls are built differently, dress differently, and are expected to have different interests and ways of behaving.

Religious Development

Religious beliefs and practices often begin in the pre-school period. The religion of these little children is:

1. *The Result of Religious Education* What he is taught at home and in church will influence his thinking. Small children are accustomed to accepting the pronouncements of adults and they usually do not question what they are told about God. The more training a child has had, the more he will feel a need for religion as he grows older (Jersild, 1952). It must be remembered, however, that little children have very limited understanding and terms like "savior," "cross," or "love" are meaningless. To be effective, therefore, religious training must be suited to the child's level of understanding, non-authoritarian, and related to his experiences.

2. *Based on Common Experience* His experiences in church and his observation of religious practices in the home will determine how the child views religion. Words don't mean much, but experiences do. A "loving heavenly Father" is foolishness if the child's earthly father is harsh and unkind. Even the child's views of God, Heaven, angels, and Hell are in terms of pictures he has seen. Such pictures can distort the child's thinking as illustrated in an oft-quoted

statement by Murphy (1956). For many children Jesus is pictured

> ...not as an ideal grown-up who helped people, but as a little baby whose mother put him in a straw thing in a barn instead of a crib, and to whom queer-looking men in striped gowns brought presents no baby could use. They learn, too, that there was a bad king, with a ferocious face, of whom the baby's mother was afraid, so that she had to take him a long way from home, riding on an animal that is not seen in the city, not even in the zoo.

As the child grows older and has different experiences and more mature understanding, his religious conceptions also change.

3. *Self-centered* Children sometimes conceive of God as "an absent-minded magician, given to granting any thoughtless petition" (Jersild, 1968). Prayers and worship are viewed as ways of getting what one wants, rather than petitions for help to act in accordance with God's desires. This view of religion as a means to selfish ends, carries over into grade school (Freeman, 1931) and may be the basis for the later doubts which occur when requests are not granted. Early in life children must learn that prayer is not a convenient rabbit's foot, but is instead a merging of our will with God's.

Before leaving this topic, something should be said about moral behavior. Concepts of right and wrong in preschoolers are learned, for the most part, from parents. Parental example is important and so are the parent's actions. By punishment or with-holding rewards when the child is bad, and by giving rewards for good behavior, parents mold the moral behavior of their children.

Potential Problems

At any stage in life, the potential problems could be legion. Typical preschool difficulties such as persistent thumbsucking, rebellious behavior, intense emotional reactions, problems with toilet training, and other issues are discussed elsewhere (Ilg & Ames, 1955). In this section we will limit ourselves to two issues that are of more direct concern to church leaders: what to tell a child about Santa Claus, and the problems of facing crises.

Concerning *Santa Claus,* we must recognize that little children love and probably need fantasy. Fantasies help them to face the perplexities of life and to make their worlds exciting and wonderful. To rob a young person of fantasy, therefore, is to rob him of much of the joy of childhood.

The person and work of Santa Claus is a childhood fantasy that most preschoolers accept without a trace of doubt. Whether or not such belief is harmful is an issue over which psychologists, parents and Christians often disagree. In the author's opinion Christian parents should not encourage their children to believe in Santa Claus since this mythical creature has been given many of the attributes of God. He is the giver of good and perfect gifts, the source of greatest happiness, and a judge who gives rewards to those who have been good. He is omniscient ("he sees you when you're sleeping, he knows when you're awake) omnipresent ("he knows if you've been bad or good") and omnipotent (since he is the only human who can fly without mechanical help, carry tons of toys on one sleigh, and enter millions of homes in the course of a few hours). For many children, even in Christian homes, Santa Claus, has become an idol that has replaced the Christ of Christmas.

Christian parents must decide for themselves whether they agree with the above interpretation and whether they should encourage belief in Santa Claus. For those who want to de-emphasize the Santa Claus myth, an explanation such as the following can be given.

> Santa Claus is a man dressed up in funny Christmas clothes. Some children believe he brings presents, but the toys that appear on Christmas morning are really put there by mommy and daddy. Some little children don't know that Santa Claus is just a man, so we must keep this secret in our family (Collins, 1969).

With this should come an emphasis on the real meaning of Christmas. "It is the birthday of Jesus, and because it is a birthday, we give presents."

Undoubtedly of greater importance is the issue of how children meet *crises*. For preschoolers with limited understanding and knowledge, such events as going to the dentist, being hospitalized, starting nursery school (or Sunday school), moving to a new home, or attending a birthday party, can all be very distressing.

There are several ways in which the stress of a crisis can be reduced. In language that he can understand, the child should be prepared for what is coming. He should be told what to expect and, when possible, permitted to visit the dentist, school, or new home prior to his later encounter. People whom he respects and some of the toys which give security should accompany him when possible. He should be given reassurance but should not be deceived. Doctors, dentists, teachers, and other people who work with children can often give practical advice on how to reduce the shock of a crisis, and a church leader who works with children might profit from reading a book like Sula Wolff's *Children Under Stress* (1969).

Implications for Church Leaders

Since preschoolers are so impressionable, the church leader can continue to guide and encourage parents to develop Christ-centered homes. Young children are likely to learn more about Christianity by living with and observing devoted parents than they will ever learn in church.

Parents and Sunday school teachers should always be aware of the child's level of understanding. Difficult concepts should be postponed and teaching should be simple and meaningful. In some Sunday schools the Bible story is repeated two or three times (in succeeding weeks) for very young children. Preschoolers enjoy such repetition and remember because of it. When there is a period of free play, use of music with singing and accompanying actions, a change to draw or act out the lesson, simplified language, and a use of illustrations that are meaningful to children, the Sunday school hour for preschoolers will not be wasted.

Middle Childhood

In the years between six and twelve, the world of the child changes drastically. As a preschooler he had to adjust to the expectations of parents, relatives, and a few playmates. When he begins school, however, the youngster discovers that parents are not always around to shield and protect. Now, he must adjust to the demands of school assignments, homework, routines, teachers, and classmates. At the same time, many parents expect their children to take music lessons, participate in Little League, read library books, and engage in numerous other activities. The young people often want to succeed in these and children do not react well when they fail.

Characteristics of Middle Childhood

These social activities are of great importance during middle childhood. In this age period the child continues to grow physically, his facial features become more "adult" in appearance, and his motor skills improve. But the most pronounced, and undoubtedly the most significant changes concern his social and intellectual development.

Social development focuses largely on the child's relationships with his peers. So prevalent is this interaction that some psychologists have labeled middle childhood the "gang age."

> The school-age child spends as much of his time as possible in the company of his peers, from whom he learns at firsthand about social structures, about in-groups and out-groups, about leadership and fellowship, about justice and injustice, about loyalties and heros and ideals. But even as he becomes a member of the distinct society of children, with its own roles and rules and folkways, he also, sometimes unwittingly and sometimes grudgingly, learns the ways and standards of adult society...Among his friends, the middle-years child lives in a special culture with its own traditional games, rhymes, riddles, tricks, superstitions, factual and mythical lore, and skills, transmitted virtually intact from one childhood generation to the next, sometimes over a period of centuries, with no help from adults and often in spite of them (Stone & Church, 1968, p. 364).

School-age children enjoy chants ("Ladybug, ladybug, fly away home." "It's raining, it's pouring, the old man is snoring."), taunts ("Roses are red, violets are blue, if I had your mug, I'd be in the zoo."), games (hide and seek, marbles, jacks, hop scotch), riddles ("Why does a chicken cross the road?"), stunts (like wiggling ears, or rubbing the stomach and patting the head at the same time), tongue twisters, coded talk ("pig-latin") and the use of slang expressions that are currently in vogue with the gang. These games and rituals enable children to interact with each other and to feel accepted in a group. Often close friendships are formed, but these usually do not last very long. Sometimes one person becomes a scapegoat who is taunted, criticized and rejected by the others. Usually the school-age child plays pretty much exclusively with others of the same sex, and in this way children learn male and female roles and behavior.

When they are in groups, school age children want very much to conform to the expectations and attitudes of the others. If the group members decide to laugh and joke in Sunday school, for example, the teacher is likely to have difficulty in gaining and keeping control of the class. For the middle-age child it is more important to go along with his peers, than to risk ostracism by conforming to adult suggestions. For the adult, the trick is to sell the whole group on an idea or plan of action.

In addition to friends outside of the home, most children must also learn to get along with brothers and sisters. The way in which a school-age child reacts to older children in the home varies with the family and the nature of the children. Often there is rivalry, tattling, belittling and bantering—especially if the children are close in age. Sometimes the younger is guided and protected by the older who, at the same time, is jealous of the prerogatives of his age, and critical if the younger is not kept in his place. Regardless of the extent of internal family dissention, children almost always rise to the defense of family members if criticism comes from outside of the home. Of course, some siblings get along well as pals and even the most antagonistic have periods of smooth interpersonal relations.

Although the peer group is very important during the age of middle childhood, the parents continue to exert a significant influence in the child's development. As long as children are in the home, parents fulfill the roles of caretaking (providing food, clothing, protection, etc.), training (guiding present behavior to prepare the child for the future), and providing emotional support (in the form of love, encouragement, comfort, pride, etc.). In addition, parents are also models for children to observe and a source of stability, direction, and regulation. Parents should let children develop independence, but because of his immaturity, the child must be protected and stopped from engaging in some activities. This is a very difficult challenge for a parent: to keep hold of the reins while allowing enough freedom for the child to mature. How the mother and father will perform their roles and influence the development of school-age children depends somewhat on the size of the family, the attitudes and expectations of the parents, the socio-economic status of the home, and the affection between family members.

Once the child has begun school, parents are not the only adults who guide his social development. Teachers, leaders of church groups, scout leaders, and other adults are sometimes very influential. This can create problems if the teacher, for example, has a set of values which differs from those of the parents. Sometimes children whose parents immigrated after being raised in another country have great adjustment difficulties if the standards and expectations of the school and community differ from those of the home. This can also be a problem for missionaries who grow up in one society and bring their cultural norms, along with their Christianity, to the children in another society. Problems can also arise when parents who grew up in one era discover what their children are being taught by the "new generation."

Teachers, however, influence more than the child's social development. They are also the chief guides in *intellectual development*. By observing young children very carefully and by the use of some ingenious psychological tests, Piaget (1924, 1963, 1965) has extensively studied this area. When a child has reached school age he is able to use speech to express his thoughts. He takes in or "assimilates" information from his environment and tries to "accomodate" or fit this in to what he already knows. He begins to get some idea of time, size and space. Between the ages of seven and eleven, the child learns to classify objects in his environment (perhaps this accounts for the interest in collections), he begins to get some conception of numbers, he starts to use some logical reasoning and he acquires what Piaget calls "conservation"—the recognition that the amount of something remains the same regardless of the shape, length, color or location.[4]   As they grow older, children show increases in attention span, reading, writing ability, and vocabulary.   They also become less egocentric—able to recognize that everyone does not think like they do.

Before long, school children begin to show considerable differences in their intellectual ability.   These differences are measured by tests which often give a score known as an IQ or intelligence quotient. An IQ of 90 to 110 is considered average and while it was once commonly believed that the IQ never changes, we now realize that this is not so.   There can be considerable variation in one's IQ score, and this can be raised if the child is in an intellectually enriching environment. Children (like adults) differ not only in overall intelligence, but also in specific abilities such as reading comprehension and speed; language, music, art, and mechanical aptitude; mathematical ability; and athletic capabilities.   These differences will be very apparent to the person who works with children or has them in the home.

Religious and Moral Development

The religious development of children has not been studied systematically by psychologists.   This is primarily because spiritual growth is difficult to investigate with the study techniques of psychology.   In a review of books on childhood religion, Edwards (1969) concluded that the literature points to three conclusions: (1) Infancy and early childhood are a basic time for spiritual growth; (2) children are active learners; (3) no other influence is as strong as that of the parents (or parent figure)—when the parents fail to give guidance and serve as models, negative peer influences are likely to influence growth instead.

61

If psychologists can be accused of ignoring childhood religion, the same cannot be said about moral development. Many years ago, Freud concluded that the young child has no conception of right or wrong, but he soon discovers that parents place certain inhibitions and directions on his behavior. Since the parents have the power to reward or punish, the child begins to act in accordance with parental expectations. Before long, the child accepts as his own the parental views of what is right and wrong and these internalized moral standards become a part of the personality which Freud called the super-ego.

In the 1920's Hartshorne and May (1930) conducted a series of experimental studies dealing with moral development in children. The researchers questioned children about their views of right and wrong, observed children in tests of moral behavior, and interviewed teachers concerning the characteristics of their pupils. The results of this careful study were startling. As children grow older their knowledge of right and wrong increases, it was found, but so does their tendency to be deceptive. Indeed there was no correlation between *knowledge* of right and wrong, and moral *behavior*—a finding that was supported by the subsequent research of other experimenters. Hartshorne and May also discovered that there were no traits such as honesty, cooperation, helpfulness, or consideration which characterized a child's behavior in all situations. A child who is honest in one situation, might be dishonest in another. Children who were duller, emotionally unstable, or from lower socio-economic status homes, lagged behind in their moral development. Finally, the research revealed some interesting conclusions about the influence of Sunday school. In terms of honesty, cooperation, inhibition of undesirable behavior, and persistence, those who were *enrolled* in Sunday school showed more desirable conduct than those who were not enrolled. [5]

Jean Piaget (1932), once again, has done some of the most creative work in the area of moral development.

As children mature, Piaget found, they shift from: morals based on specific rules, to morals based on general conceptions of right and wrong; moral conduct that is in response to external standards, to that which is a response to internal standards and making judgments in terms of inflexible rules ("you should be spanked because you spilled your milk") to a willingness to consider circumstances ("you spilled your milk but it was an accident").

There is also a shift in views about justice. In one study (Harrower, 1924) children were told of two boys, Tommy and Peter, who were playing together. Tommy had an engine, and Peter had a boat. Suddenly, Tommy smashed Peter's boat. Now, the children were asked, what should be done to Tommy. Very young children appeal to authority and demand punishment while children who are older resort to retribution ("break Tommy's engine"). It is not until a later age (six years and above in children from privileged homes; eight years and above in children from poorer homes) that the idea of restitution was more common: Tommy should replace the broken boat.

All of these studies show that moral behavior is learned. The very young child tries to emulate and please his parents, to get their approval because he "is good" and to avoid punishment for "being bad." As he matures the child develops his own standards and controls—especially during the years of middle childhood and adolescence. These findings can be of great importance to parents and religious educators.

Implications For Church Leaders

The church leader can influence development during middle childhood in at least three ways.

1. Be alert to the importance of parental training. Even though the school-age child is influenced by teachers, peers, and other people outside of the home, the parents still bear a major responsibility in the child's social, emotional, intellectual, and spiritual development. In middle

childhood, youngsters need parents who are warm, thoughtful, loving, and so concerned about their children that there is discipline and some kind, but firm, standards in the home. With this awareness of the importance of parental influences, the church leader can encourage his people to create homes where Christ is pre-eminent (Colossians 1:18), where the parents have a warm relationship with each other (Ephesians 5:21-33), and where the children are trained and disciplined (Proverbs 22:6, 23:13) but not scolded and nagged so that they become angry and resentful (Ephesians 6:4, Living Letters).

2. The church, along with the parents, can guide in the child's religious and moral growth. School age children are maturing rapidly in their intellectual development and the church must be aware of this so that religious instruction can be geared to the child's current level of thinking. Pattison has stated this explicity in discussing the learning of morals.

> ...the child must be continually pushed toward the replacement of immature concepts of morality by more mature concepts as he goes through stages of moral development. Perhaps an example will illustrate the point. A four-year-old must learn most definitely that he must not cross streets against a red light. However, the ten-year-old must be taught that there is no absoluteness about red lights. Yet the ten-year-old must still respond to red lights as a meaningful and relevant directive for behavior. In other words, at different ages the same moral problem must be reevaluated in terms of its meaningfulness to the child (1969, p. 28).

3. The church leader can work with parents in dealing with some of the special problems that school-age children face. Chief among these are social adjustment, the development of self esteem, and sex education.

Social adjustment, of course, begins early and experiences in Sunday school or nursery school do much to prepare the child for later peer interactions. Nevertheless all children experience some problems in getting along with others; and for some, there are continual difficulties as they try to adapt to peer influences outside of the home. When a child has adjustment problems the parents should help him to face and express his feeling about the situation. Since children can be better helped when parents understand the child's view of the difficulties and give supportive and practical guidance, the parents should be accepting and not critical or ridiculing. Of course, a teacher is frequently a good source of information and can often give excellent practical advice about the problems of school children. The church leader also can give an outsider's viewpoint when problems arise and he is often able to encourage parents.

When a child is *rejected* by his parents, teachers or class-mates, or when he persistently fails (at least in his own eyes), he has difficulty accepting himself as a person of worth. Sometimes a low opinion of oneself comes from the parents because parents who do not have a healthy degree of self acceptance tend to raise children who are also lacking in self esteem (Coopersmith, 1967). This in turn influences the child's ability to accept and get along with others. (Perhaps this was what Jesus had in mind when He linked love of others with self-love, Matthew 19:19.) To increase a child's self acceptance, several techniques might be helpful (Hurlock, 1964). First, the child should be encouraged to set goals which are possible for him to reach. This does not mean that we should discourage ambition. It means, rather, that the child's aspirations should be realistic so that he does not experience repeated failure. Secondly, we should encourage self-understanding. The better a child understands himself, his capabilities, and his weaknesses, the better is he able to accept himself. Thirdly, we should encourage others to accept the child. Certainly it is hard to accept yourself if others reject you. Jesus accepted everyone—even the unlovely—although He didn't always accept their behavior. Christian parents and church members must do the same. This acceptance by others, however, should be consistent. It is hard for a child to feel accepted if he gets favorable treatment at one time and unfavorable treatment at other times. Even when children are being disciplined, parents can show that they accept and love the child, in spite of his undesirable behavior.

Then there is the issue of *sex*. Parents are sometimes embarrassed and uncertain about how to proceed when questions on this topic arise. If the topic is avoided or the queries are unanswered, the child is likely to seek information from peers or elsewhere and this often results in knowledge that is inaccurate and misleading. The best guideline for parents is to answer children's questions truthfully and in language that can be understood. Parents should give enough information to answer his immediate question (don't try to cover the entire topic of sex at one time) and the issue should be discussed in a matter-or-fact fashion. It is best to use correct names for body parts (such as penis or vagina) and children should be told in advance about such predictable happenings as erections, nocturnal emissions (wet dreams) or menstration.[6]

Summary

The period of time covered in this chapter—from conception to the beginning of adolescence—is crucial in human development. During this period the child makes great strides in terms of his physical maturation; social, intellectual and emotional development; and spiritual growth. Although behavior can be changed at any time in life, the early years always play a significant part in molding the attitudes and behavior of adulthood.

The present chapter has described some of the typical developmental events that occur during the nine months prior to birth, during infancy, in the preschool years, and during the period of middle childhood. An understanding of these normal processes of development can be of great value to the church leader as he counsels with parents and their children, prepares messages on the Christian home, and guides the development of an effective children's Christian Education program.

Chapter Three

ADOLESCENCE: THE TUMULTUOUS YEARS

Adolescence is a period of time between late childhood and the late teens when young people are casting off their childish ways and growing into adulthood. This is a period of social development, increasing independence, sexual maturation, and great physical growth. It is a time for deciding on one's purpose in life and beginning to find one's identity. It is also a time of conflict and stress—at least in modern western society—as individuals struggle to acquire the skills, privileges and responsibilities of adulthood.

Parents and church leaders are often frustrated in their attempts to understand what teenagers are really like. Adolescents severely criticize their parents, but sometimes become childlike in their dependence. They condemn church leaders and giggle in the services, but they often show intense religious concerns. They want to be adults, but their fashions, hair styles, slang, music, interests, and tribal-like dances are a constant source of amazement to the "over thirty generation." They want to be understood and accepted, but they are often criticized instead. According to one writer, young people "love luxury. They have bad manners, contempt for authority, disrespect for elder people.... They contradict their parents, chatter before company, gobble their food, and tyrannize their teachers." When we consider that this contemporary sounding statement was written many centuries ago by Plato, it is clear that the problem of understanding and appreciating adolescence is very old.

After surveying several thousand adolescents, two researchers from Purdue University summarized the complexities of this time of life.

> This, then is the modern teenager: a boy or girl whose energies are already sapped by the sheer process of physical growth, caught up in a whirl of school work and social activities in and out of school, confronted by decisions which will affect his entire life, confused by the shifting attitudes of parents, teachers and society in general, all of whom doubt him and his behavior—and bewildered by the complex and rapidly changing civilization into which he must soon fit, assuming all of the responsibilities of maturity (Remmers and Radler, 1957, p. 50).

For the church worker who is involved with teenagers, it is important to be familiar with the most commonly observed characteristics and problems of these young people, and to know something about their attitudes towards religion. All of these will be considered in this chapter. Although we will make some summary statements about "typical adolescents," it must be remembered that teenagers—like every other age-group—show large individual differences. Every adolescent faces biological change and strong cultural pressures, but no two adolescents experience and react to these in exactly the same way.

Adolescent Characteristics

The adolescent in our society must achieve independence and identity as he moves toward adulthood. In accomplishing this, he has to find new ways of relating to parents, peers, and society at large. He must learn to date, to think like an adult, to plan for his future, and to decide on his values and religious beliefs. Probably the first major adjustment of adolescence, however, concerns the physical changes that occur during this period.

Physical Changes

In the early years of adolescence (roughly between eleven and fifteen) the pituitary gland, situated in the brain, secretes hormones which result in such significant physical changes as a rapid growth in body size and a maturation of the reproductive system.

The so-called "growth-spurt" of adolescence refers to an accelerated increase in both height and weight. For boys, the most rapid period of growth tends to occur at about age fourteen; for girls it is around age twelve. (In most of these physical changes, girls develop faster than boys.) There are large individual differences in the growth spurt, however, and it is not unusual to find two normal thirteen-year-olds, for example, who are literally "head and shoulders" apart in height. There are also differences in the extent to which puberal fat accumulates during early adolescence. This only persists for a couple of years and usually disappears when hormone balance is restored, but a problem of over-weight can be very distressing to a body-conscious teenager. More welcome, perhaps, are the changes in body proportions. The head, which was one-fourth of the body length at birth, becomes smaller in proportion to the total body length. (In adulthood, the head is about one-eighth the body length). The facial features lose their baby look, the legs change in length and shape, and there is a growth in the size and capacity of the lungs. It should not be surprising that during this time of rapid body growth, there is also an increase in the amount of food which is desired, needed, and consumed. Parents of teenagers are well aware of this fact, but it is sometimes overlooked by church leaders who plan "refreshments" for teenage social events.

Sexual changes in adolescence can be classified into two categories: primary and secondary. Primary sex changes concern the reproductive organs. In males the penis, testes, and other parts of the reproductive system enlarge in size and mature in function. At some time between ages twelve and sixteen, nocturnal emissions (wet dreams) begin to occur in which the male experiences an erection and involuntary ejaculation of semen during his sleep. Often he is unaware that this has happened until he sees the spot on the sheets or on his pajamas in the morning. While this is a natural occurrence, many boys do not realize what is happening and are too embarassed to ask about it or to mention it to anyone else.

In the female, since most of the reproductive organs lie within the body, growth is not so easily observed. There is sometimes an embarassing enlargement of the abdomen but this disappears as the bones grow and make sufficient space for the enlarged organs. The functioning of the female reproductive system is signaled by the menarche — the first menstration. This does not signal complete sexual maturity but instead initiates a period, lasting anywhere from one month to several years, during which the adolescent has a menstrual flow but is sterile and unable to conceive a child (Hurlock, 1967). For the girl who knows in advance about menstration, its coming may be welcomed as a further sign of advancing adulthood. The girl who has not been prepared for the menarche, however, is often horrified when it occurs. This horror sometimes persists for life so that menstration is always dreaded and feared. This is especially likely if the periods are accompanied by pain and other physical discomfort. Other girls experience emotional upsets during menstration, inability to study, embarassment, and sometimes resentment. A sympathetic and supportive adult can do much to influence a young girl's attitude as she experiences these and other sexual changes.

Secondary sex characteristics are those physical features which signal adulthood but are not directly concerned with the reproductive organs. Both sexes develop pubic hair, and (especially in boys) hair on the face, chest, and other parts of the body. In both sexes, the voice pitch lowers, the skin becomes coarser, and the glands produce an oily secretion which often leads to blackheads, pimples and body odors. In girls, the breasts develop and hips broaden; while in boys there is broadening of the trunk and shoulders.

All of these physical changes can have a psychological influence on the young teenager. The growth spurt is sometimes followed by a humiliating clumsiness which persists until the adolescent gets accustomed to his longer limbs. The appearance of fuzz on the face, the change in body proportions, the "cracking voice," pimples, and body odors can all be additional causes of embarassment. Since tall broad shouldered men and petite shapely women seem to be the ideal in our society, young people who do not meet these standards are often distressed because for them it is very important to be physically attractive. Even the time of these changes seems to be important. Studies show that boys whose physical maturation occurs later than average, feel inadequate, rejected, dominated, socially awkward, and rebellious. Some of these feelings may even persist into adulthood (Jones & Bayley, 1950; Mussen & Jones, 1957). Likewise, late maturing girls tend to think less of themselves, have more worries, are slower to develop interests in boys, and have less concern about personal "adornment and display" (Stone & Barker, 1939; Jones & Mussen, 1958). It should be added, however, that many of these adverse psychological effects do not appear when the teenager has understanding accepting parents and re-warding social contacts with others.

Independence and Identity

As he grows into adulthood, the adolescent must launch out on his own, establishing independence from his parents and a self-identity. The whole society encourages this and looks with disapproval at the individual who is too long "tied to his mother's apron strings." But the society also erects obstacles which prevent complete independence. The need for lengthy schooling (which results in a more

73

prolonged financial dependence on the parents), the importance of delaying marriage (which often keeps the young person living at home), and the reluctance of parents to "let go," all delay independence (Mussen, Conger, & Kagan, 1969).

According to Erik Erikson, the famous Harvard psychoanalyst, becoming independent is important, but it is not the central problem in adolescence—finding a "sense of identity" is of greater significance. The young person must ask: "Who am I?" "What are my values?" "What is my purpose for living?" "What are my goals in life?" "Where am I going?" "What are my strengths and weaknesses?" For most people the teenage years are a time of searching for answers to questions such as these and of experimenting with behavior that will help to develop a clear self-picture (Erikson, 1963, 1968). This is a difficult task and it is because of this, according to Erikson, that society frees the adolescent from adult responsibilities for a few years, in order that he can have opportunity to form his identity. During this time the church, with its emphases on values and guidelines for living, can be of great help to young people as they search for a place in life. Bible study and discussion groups can be geared to the recognition and discussion of identity problems.

Social Development

In achieving independence and formulating one's identity, social relationships with parents, peers, and society at large are very important.

Parents of teenagers usually desire the best for their children. Such parents recognize the importance of a child's becoming independent but at the same time they want to protect the children from corruption. This raises the challenge of "letting the reins slacken at the right time and in the right way, neither holding them so tightly that the child resists nor releasing them so suddenly as to endanger him" (Douvan & Adelson, 1966, p. 163). Since a balance such as this is almost impossible for parents to achieve consistently, parent-child conflicts during adolescence often increase. These conflicts fall into two main categories: (1) issues involving adolescent demands for greater independence than the parents are willing to grant, and (2) issues involving parental intolerance of what they perceive to be childish and immature behavior in the teenagers (Mussen, Conger, & Kagan, 1969).

Let us first deal with the latter of these two issues. Parents are reluctant to trust teenagers and give them added independence if the adolescent consistently displays noisiness, teasing of siblings, untidiness, silliness and shirking of home duties. Outlandish (from the parents' point of view) clothing, hair styles and tastes in music or art can also be a source of conflict. When young people advocate views of religion, sex, morals, or politics that contrast with what they have learned at home, there is a tendency for parents to assume (sometimes with justification) that the teenager has "not thought through" the issue. The problem is accentuated if the parents disagree among themselves or are inconsistent concerning their views of adolescent behavior. This leaves the young person not knowing what to expect or where he stands.

Probably more common, however, are the conflicts over parental unwillingness to meet adolescent demands. Table 3-1 summarizes the most frequent complaints that teenagers have against their parents. To this list might be added conflicts over when the teen gets in at night, use of the family car, or freedom to choose one's friends and beliefs. Sometimes teenagers also feel that parents are highly inconsistent. "They tell you you're old enough to take out the garbage, tidy your room, hold a part-time job and act like an adult," the young person complains, "but then they say you're not old enough to stay out late or they don't trust you to use the car." Of course, parents could also produce an equally impressive statement of their complaints which could be listed as a parallel to Table 3-1.

Table 3—1

Most Common Teenage Complaints Against Parents*

1. Adults refuse to recognize that teenagers are human beings with feelings, dignity and pride of their own.

2. Teenagers claim that parents often fail to observe even the most elementary rules of courtesy. For example, they often think nothing of scolding their children in front of friends.

3. "Sometimes parents act as if you weren't even alive." One girl said, "You'll be sitting right there in a roomful of company and your parents will start talking about you. You're supposed to sit there as if you were a little machine or something."

4. Parents also seem to have a special knack for embarrassing teenagers in front of their dates.

5. Parents are completely contemptuous of their property rights. They assume that no teenager really can own anything, that adults are the sole owners of everything in the family, the supreme givers who can also take away.

6. Even the best parents have a tendency to meddle far too much in the romances of their children.

7. On social matters, too many mothers and fathers consider it a personal reflection if their sons and daughters are not good mixers.

8. Overambitious fathers and mothers expect too much of their children. Often the complaint centers around the report card.

9. Parents have a way of making their decisions and issuing their edicts without really thinking about the effect on their sensitive youngsters.

10. Many parents insist that their children are going to grow up by their golden rules, regardless of what everybody else is doing.

11. Teenagers often feel that privacy is denied them.

*Adapted from E. Havemann, "The Teen-Agers Case Against Parents," *McCalls,* November, 1956, pp . 45 f.

76

Many of the parent-teen conflicts are accentuated by a lack of communication. Often there is no serious attempt or desire on either side to understand, appreciate or respect the other's point of view. Frequently the parents interact with their friends; the teenagers spend most of their time with their peer group, and there is little real effort to discuss issues meaningfully within the family setting. The much discussed "generation gap" becomes even wider when rapid social and cultural change gives the parents and their offspring different experiences so that they have very little in common. In addition lack of communication may result from inexperience. When family members have learned to talk over their problems, the home life is happier (Slocum, 1958), but unfortunately, many families have never discussed significant issues and it is hard to begin when teenagers are struggling for independence.

The *peer* group also creates a strong social influence during the high school years. The adolescent wants to break away from home, but he often finds that this process is very painful. To help make the break easier and to give security while he is doing so, the teenager often associates with others of about the same age, who are also moving out from under parental domination. The group bands together. Slavish adherence to the latest fads in dress, language, interest, and music become very important because this gives the gang solidarity and helps the individual to be accepted by the "in-group." Since it is also important to be noticed, teenagers engage in a lot of loud talking and other attention-seeking behavior. (The church worker who tries to keep an adolescent group "under control" knows this.) When the group is not together at school, in church, or near some "hangout," the members often communicate for hours on the telephone.

In addition to providing security, the peer group helps its members in other ways. The gang provides opportunity for companionship; permits the release of emotional tensions through "kibitzing" and the discussion of fears or

77

other tensions; gives the adolescent opportunity to learn and practice social skills; helps him to develop tolerance and understanding; sets some guiding rules of behavior while he is rebelling against adult standards and formulating his own values; provides opportunities for fun; is a source of status; and provides opportunity for interaction and "comparing notes" with others who are growing to adulthood (Hurlock, 1967).

Of course, peer influences are not always beneficial. Individuality can be stifled by membership in a group; envy and frustration can occur when young people "can't keep up with the teenage Joneses"; the adolescent who is left out feels unhappy and rejected; and gangs sometimes form for the purpose of carrying out acts of violence and destruction. Because we recognize that conformity to peer group standards is associated with good psychological adjustment, there is danger in assuming that the non-conformist is somehow maladjusted. This need not be so, since non-conformists are often very creative and might discover that conformity to a group squelches their ability and individuality. It is important, nevertheless, for every adolescent to experience at least some peer influences (Langner 1954).

The teenage group often accentuates differences between adolescents and their parents. "But everyone else is doing it," and similar complaints are used in an attempt to force parents to yield to the standards of the group. When the parents refuse, there are problems. Some parents, rather than taking a firm stand, become overly concerned about their children's social adjustment and always let the teenager have his way. Other parents try to be pals—dressing, talking and acting like their teenage offspring, but failing to recognize that young people do not appreciate this kind of parental behavior. In spite of their rebellion, teenagers want mothers and fathers to be parents who can provide stability, encouragement, protection, standards and advice when needed.

Early in adolescence, peer relationships are mostly with others of the same sex. Later, interests develop in the opposite sex and before long, dating begins. Since dating behavior must be learned, young teenagers are much concerned about how they should act in the presence of the opposite sex. Our society has such varied dating and sexual standards, however, that the teenager frequently has no clear-cut guidelines to indicate what is desirable or permissible. This uncertainty is typical of teenagers within the church as well as those without. In their study of 3000 high school seniors in evangelical churches, Zuck and Getz (1968) found that more help was desired on dating and marriage than on any other topic.

Dating influences behavior in several ways. It provides an opportunity for learning how to relate socially to the opposite sex; it is a chart of one's popularity, success and reputation; it can build self-confidence and teach an individual about oneself; it can be an opportunity for learning how to communicate; it permits a formulation of ideas concerning what one seeks in a mate; and later it is the channel through which one finds a spouse. In the United States, this dating begins at about age fourteen, but there is evidence to show, that such early dating may not be wise. Since our society does not believe in chaperones, young people are "on their own" when they date. The car provides almost unlimited freedom and the adolescent whose sexual characteristics are just developing sometimes is unable to control his passions. Often, early dating leads to pregnancies and teenage marriages, about half of which end in divorce. Even going steady may be unwise in early adolescence. At least two studies have found that teenagers who went steady, wished in retrospect that they had not. While going steady is sometimes encouraged by parents and sanctioned by peers, such behavior makes sexual behavior more likely, isolates and retards development of social skills, and deprives one of close friendships with peers of the same sex (Martinson, 1966; Douvan & Adelson, 1966).

No dating during adolescence is equally undesirable. A study of teenage girls showed that

> ...the late adolescent who has not yet begun to date presents a picture of pervasive psychological problems. She is not only retarded in social development vis-a-vis her peers, but shows signs of poor development in all areas of social interaction. Here we find a girl who is overly dependent on the family, who is insecure and self-absorbed, who knows clearly that she is out of phase with her own age group and is worried about her deviance...(Her) conceptions of like-sexed friendships are equally immature (Douvan & Adelson, 1966, p. 218).

Apparently, it is desirable for adolescents to get to know many people of both sexes, before extensive dating and going steady begins.

Of course, the adolescent's social activities are not confined to his family and friends. He lives in a *society* and must learn to interact with the broader community of which he is a member. Sometimes, the adolescent reacts against the society with acts of juvenile delinquency or political violence. More often, he is interested in the community and wants to be responsibly involved. According to one writer, there is evidence that

> ...with the decline in size and function of the family unit, forces within the community have assumed a more important role; consequently, at some point, the growing individual comes face to face with problems that are not solved on the basis of authority or of sentiment, as are problems arising at home.... The adolescent must be given an opportunity to make social contacts outside the home and immediate neighborhood, to accept responsibility, and to display a reasonable amount of initiative in order to develop the personal and social self (Garrison, 1965, p. 326).

The community—including the schools, churches, and youth groups—provides standards of behavior, and moral guidelines for young people. Many prejudices, likes, dislikes, tastes, attitudes, and cultural interests are a reflection of the community and neighborhood in which the adolescents live (Garrison, 1965). In turn, teenagers have an influence on the community both by involvement in worthy neighborhood projects and by boosting the economy as they spend about twelve billion dollars per year—mostly on luxury items. According to an estimate made by *Newsweek* magazine (March 21, 1966) teenagers buy forty-five per cent of all soft drinks, eighty-one per cent of all single phonograph records, thirty per cent of low priced cameras, twenty-four per cent of wristwatches, twenty per cent of all radios, and sixteen per cent of all cosmetics. Girls alone, spend at least two billion dollars a year on clothes.

Although teenagers look to the society for guidance, adolescents are often treated as a minority group that is the object of discrimination, prejudice and segregation. In the United States and Canada the society makes no real place for the adolescent but instead reacts to him with criticism, mistrust, denial of privileges or responsibilities, and sometimes fear. Apparently, like parents, society at large (including the church) is unsure of the extent to which adolescents can be trusted with responsibilities. This is often frustrating to the teenagers who thus react as do all minority groups—by forming their own society and turning to each other for support (Kalish, 1966). Happily, efforts are now being made to enlist adolescents more fully into church, school, and community affairs (Wright, 1959).

Sexual Behavior

The growth of primary and secondary sex characteristics in adolescence brings with it an increased desire for sexual gratification. This desire is accentuated by the society's preoccupation with sex. Movies, television, literature, advertisements, and the sexually liberal attitudes of peers, adults and advocates of the new morality stimulate adolescents and lead to confusion as they seek to formulate personal moral standards.

In dealing with his sexual urges, the adolescent must face two problems. He must learn to live with and control his heightened impulses, and he must develop a personal set of moral standards (Douvan & Adelson, 1966). He may fail in both of these tasks, succeed in both, or succeed in only one. An example of the latter is the person who decides that premarital intercourse is bad, but who cannot seem to stop himself from engaging in this behavior.

There are three ways in which adolescents (and those who are older) give expression to their sexual impulses: through "homoerotic activity," through self-stimulation, and through contacts with the opposite sex.

Homoeroticism is to be strongly attracted to and/or attached to members of one's own sex. In early adolescence this is quite normal and very common. It may take the form of crushes or hero worship and it is especially frequent when members of the same sex live together—as in reformatories or boarding schools. Such behavior can be considered immature, however, and it is usually outgrown by the late teens. If, as he grows into adulthood, a person continues to desire sexual pleasure from members of his own sex, the term "homosexual" is used. This is a more abnormal condition that will be discussed further in another volume of this series.

Self-stimulation most often means masturbation—the stimulation of one's own genitals by stroking, fondling or playing. This is especially common in adolescent males and is almost universally practiced. Such behavior is not harmful physically but it can, and often does, lead to guilt, shame, and emotional turmoil. It is a self-centered form of gratification which usually passes, especially when the individual enters into the privileges of marriage. Although

82

it is not mentioned in the Scripture [1] it is frequently condemned by churchmen, but practiced in secret by most male adolescents. It is only when the practice persists as an adult compulsion, that masturbation indicates psychological immaturity or sexual maladjustment (Babbage, 1963).

Heterosexual activities are those involving sexual contacts with the opposite sex. Since girls mature earlier, their interest in boys begins as early as thirteen or fourteen. Boys are slower to develop heterosexual interests and it is not until they are fifteen or sixteen that most males show an open interest in girls. With both sexes heterosexual activities usually begin with "puppy love"—a stage which is awkward, bungling, playful and similar to the behavior of young puppies. During this time, adolescents are learning how to converse with members of the opposite sex, how to act in social situations, how to date, how to be attractive, and how to perform skills like dancing or adolescent sports. As they learn—usually by trial and error—the adolescents' actions are frequently silly, loud, aggressive, or in bad taste. There is often conspicuous "show-off" behavior and sometimes intense "love" affairs develop which distract the teenager from everything else and usually end in heartbreaking collapse. All of these experiences combine to create greater self-confidence, an increased ability to relate socially, and discovery of the qualities that one likes in members of the opposite sex (Hurlock, 1967).

Early in adolescence, expressions of affection are mainly non-physical. As the teenager grows older and the sex drive increases, however, affection is expressed in physical as well as non-physical ways. Dr. Elizabeth Hurlock (1967) has summarized the ways in which adolescents most commonly show their feelings for one another. They include:

1. Services for the Loved One. The adolescent enjoys giving gifts, entertainment or help.

2. Keepsakes. These can involve any item that serves as a reminder of good times together (such as a program from some football game or play that was seen together) or some prized article that the one person gives to the other "to remember me by."

3. Constant Association. This includes not only dating, but eating, studying, playing and walking together. All of this is supplemented by long talks on the telephone.

4. Confidential Discussions. Young people like to share their joys, sorrows, hopes, goals, frustrations, and feelings with each other. They also like to tell same-sex confidants of their feelings for the loved one.

5. Creative Expression. This refers to writing poetry or love letters, composing music, painting pictures or simply daydreaming as an expression of one's feelings.

6. Jealousy. This accompanies most adolescent romances. Challengers are criticized verbally and often become the object of many derogatory comments.

7. Necking. This term refers to physical intimacy which does not go lower than the neck. This always involves kissing and may include stroking of the hair or face.

8. Petting. According to Kinsey (1953) petting involves "any sort of physical contact which does not involve union of the genitalia but in which there is a deliberate attempt to effect erotic arousal." Undoubtedly this is much more common today than formerly—especially in the middle and upper socioeconomic groups. It gives sexual satisfaction, often assures one's continued popularity, and is a way of testing one's sexual capacity. If carried too far so that the participants become involved in sexual intercourse or other guilt-producing behavior, petting can also lead to a lot of unhappiness (Reevy, 1959).

9. Premarital Intercourse. This behavior, which appears to be on the increase, is often impulsive and unplanned, the uncontrollable culmination of extensive petting. When intercourse before marriage is intentional, the reasons for

such activity may include curiosity (to see what it is like), a reaction to boredom, a desire to prove one's adulthood, or a desire for status (with the sex partner or with one's peers). Some teenagers, want a premarital pregnancy so they can hurt their parents or trap a partner into marriage. Others, impressed with the "playboy philosophy," conclude that intercourse apart from marriage is acceptable, because "sex is pleasant, God-given, and to be used." Such a view forgets that desirable things must always be controlled, including guns, drugs,[2] eating, elimination—and sex. Rather than preparing one for marriage (as some young people claim), premarital sex often brings guilt, and creates a suspicion which interferes with marital happiness. Based on twenty-five years of clinical experience, one psychologist has concluded that

> ...the effects of sexual promiscuity on boys' and girls' personalities, and on their prospects of good mental health and marital adjustment, constitute more than adequate grounds for making continence prior to the marriage relationship a valid and desirable objective of sex education (Staton, 1968, p. 256).

The Bible speaks in favor of male-female companionship (Genesis 2:18), marriage (I Corinthians 7:2,9; Hebrews 13:4), and sex (Genesis 2:24; Hebrews 13:4). Sex outside of marriage is forbidden, however, (I Corinthians 7:1,2; I Thessalonians 2:4). This is not because God is a spoilsport. When He says "no" it is for the benefit of His creatures. Unanswered prayers and the presence of problems, for example, work to bring spiritual edification and growth (James 1:3; Psalm 94:12; Proverbs 3:11, 12). Likewise the control of sexual impulses prior to marriage is ultimately for our good and leads to better relationships —sexual and otherwise—within marriage.

While parents, schools, churches, and youth leaders are coming to recognize the importance of guiding adolescents as they mature sexually, there is still evidence that young people want and need more information than they are getting (Fleming and Fleming, 1970). Instead of giving the needed facts and teaching values about sex, however, adults are too often engaged in arguing about the benefits or dangers of sex education and blaming each other for the widespread moral decline in the society. Embarassed parents sometimes retreat to the safety of giving pat answers and leave it to the church or school to give more specific instruction. The churches complain that schools are teaching sex facts but with no moral standards. The schools, in turn, respond that separation of church and state requires that there be no public instruction in morality. In the meantime, adolescents continue getting inaccurate information and attitudes about sex from their peers or from pornographic literature.

The debate over sex education doubtless will persist for some time and as this continues, Christians must make their opinions heard. In a succinct appraisal of the subject, the editor of *Christianity Today* magazine recently suggested some guidelines that might be of help to parents and church leaders as they seek to impart sex information and plan programs of sex education.

> What are the minimum standards for sex-education courses that will satisfy the Christian who takes his life and world view from the biblical revelation?
>
> First and foremost, sex need not and should not be taught in isolation. Instruction should deal with the whole area of love, courtship, marriage, family, and society; sex should be treated as only a part of that total package....
>
> Moreover, children should be taught the facts of life only when they are old enough and mature enough

to accept them without psychological harm or undue embarrassment. Even teenagers do not need to be given detailed information about all aspects of the sexual relationship. Some things can wait for the post-high-school years and the approach of marriage. Sex is a very personal and intimate matter, and those who feel the urge to tell all in the supposed interest of candor and honesty should remember that the law of love may transcend candor and honesty at this point. Not all inhibitions are bad.

The part of family-life instruction that deals with the sex act should be taught to young people in separate classes. Some if not many students are totally unprepared for open discussion in mixed groups; to be placed in such a situation would cause them great embarrassment and perhaps real harm.

Sex cannot be presented in a moral vacuum. A school that allows its students to be taught that extra-marital sex is a matter of personal choice or that no moral standards are binding is bound to create havoc for them. Moral principles are the cement that holds a culture together; history affords numerous examples of nations that collapsed and disintegrated when moral principles were set aside....

Since sex is inextricably linked with morality and religion, sex-education classes should not be mandatory for all children. Parents have an inalienable right to decide whether their children should be exposed to this teaching, particularly since the programs will always vary widely from community to community....

Given the present situation, what can Christians do about sex education?

First, Christians should get involved in their local schools. They can do this through the PTA. They can review the books and other materials used in sex-education courses. They can try to persuade school administrators, elected school-board members, and even teachers, to maintain standards that do not violate biblical teaching. Parents have a high stake in their children's education and should have a determinative voice in what they are taught....

Secondly, parents owe it to their children to instruct them in the home, by example as well as by precept. If they themselves lack information, they should get it. Concerned parents can establish their own teaching classes, bringing in well-informed instructors who can help them learn what they need to present to their children.

Thirdly, Christian parents should see that their churches provide sex-education classes as part of the Christian education program....(Lindsell, 1970, pp. 12-13).

The type of church program that is started should be planned cooperatively by parents, church leaders, young married couples and some of the teenagers in the congregation. The subject matter may vary from church to church but in addition to imparting biological knowledge, there must be open consideration of teenage attitudes and problems concerning sex, along with a consideration of the biblical references to sex and marriage.

Values and Attitudes

To understand and work with adolescents, one must know something about the values, attitudes, and opinions of this age group. Such factors are often at the basis of much teenage behavior and thinking.

The formation of values is an important part of growing up. "The youngster must construct an individual...system of values and moral conduct which . . . is his own . . . not a simple copy of what he has been told to believe, but rather a guide to conduct and valuation appropriate to his own circumstances" (Douvan & Adelson, 1966, p. 79). Many of his values result from home, school, church, and community influences. Parents who are hypercritical and believe that people are not to be trusted, for example, usually have children who develop the same attitudes.

Many teenage values are also derived from the peer-group. When these do not agree with parental, church, or other "establishment" values, there will be conflict between the generations. In an analysis of the values expressed in music which is popular among teenagers, Benson (1969) concluded that the "now generation" shows no reverence for the past (and feels quite free to reject the "sacred cows" of the family); believes that man must find a meaning for existing, and must respect other individuals as persons, relishes spontaneous personal experience; rejects the puritan work ethic; opposes war; and rebels against a society which tends to dehumanize people. Sometimes such attitudes lead to cynicism mixed with periodic idealism (Eisenman, 1968).

Parents and other adults who seek to control the behavior of adolescents and guide in the formation of values and attitudes tend to use one of three methods. *Authoritarian control* is based on the assumption that adults know best and that young people must conform to the specified standards. *Permissive control* usually stems from the idea that adolescents should be free to manage their own affairs. Thus the young person is allowed to do as he pleases—even if this violates adult standards. *Democratic control* involves child-adult discussions concerning standards, coupled with attempts at mutual understanding. This latter method has five characteristics: first, there is the belief that the young person should know what is expected and why; second, before administering punishment, there is a willingness to consider reasons for violations; third, there is punishment only when the violation was deliberate; fourth, severity of the punishment is in accordance with the seriousness of the act; and fifth, punishment is closely related to the act and not designed to embarass or humiliate (Hurlock, 1967). It is perhaps not surprising that democratic disciplinarians have a greater influence over adolescents, and receive more respect and loyalty.

Interests

Just as play is important for young children, so in adolescence recreational interests and activities have a significant influence on physical health, mental well-being, and social status. These teenage years are often very busy. In an attempt to be "well-rounded," to be popular with peers, to satisfy their curiosity and to discover their real interests and abilities, adolescents are often involved in a large variety of activities. Sports, music lessons, church groups, part-time jobs, dating, school clubs, and perhaps a number of personal interests—such as reading, TV viewing, or hobbies—keep the teenager in a perpetual state of busyness. Even when he has strong religious interests, the adolescent doesn't have a lot of time for a complicated church youth program.

Future Aspirations

When a young person reaches adolescence, he realizes that he is approaching adulthood and must make some plans for the future. As he continues to mature intellectually (a point which religious educators should always remember) he begins to think about the competition for getting into college. School becomes a struggle for grades and for information which will help him pass the college admission tests. Although their conclusions may be a little extreme, there is much truth in the following statement by Stone and Church (1968, p. 506):

> Nowhere are the shortcomings of our educational system more flagrantly apparent than in the secondary

> schools...There is little concern for *personal education*, for deepening and enriching the person's understanding of himself and the world which he lives in...Class work is isolated from adolescent interests and social life. Most adolescents consider schooling a form of penal servitude, and pointless...

except as a stepping stone to a diploma, further schooling, and a better paying job.

Many teenagers are convinced that it is important to select a vocation early, and they are distressed to discover that this is such a difficult and frustrating task. In increasing numbers, high school guidance counselors are being trained to assist young people as they anticipate future vocations, but these trained counselors are still rare, and often overworked. As a result, the adolescent must usually be content with either no counseling or with a short interview or two. It is perhaps not surprising that many teenagers are looking to the church for vocational guidance (Zuck and Getz, 1968).

In addition to thoughts about future work, adolescents also look forward to marriage and think about what they would like in a future mate (Bell, 1968). Among the desirable characteristics are mental and physical fitness, desire for children, dependability, compatible interests, good personal appearance and manner, pleasant disposition, and a sense of humor. Boys want wives who can cook and keep house. Girls want husbands who make money and succeed in their vocations (Remmers, Drucker, & Christenson, 1950). Christian young people should seek mates who are also believers.

In our society, adolescence is clearly a time of rapid, often tumultous, change and growth. In addition to all of the behavior which has been summarized above, the adolescent's personality is being formulated during the teenage years, he is learning how to experience and express emotion,

and he is undergoing significant religious changes.   It is
to these religious factors that we now turn.

Adolescent Religion

   Religion involves both belief and practice. As a child, the
individual uncritically accepts his parents' beliefs and par-
ticipates in their religious rituals, but with the coming
adolescence, this changes.   The teenager is struggling
toward maturity, trying to find his own values, and attempting to get out from under parental control. In so doing, he
often takes a critical look at the "old time religion" that he
was taught in Sunday school or at home. Slowly his beliefs
may change, his religious behavior may be different, and his
attitudes towards the church and its members may alter.

Adolescent Religious Beliefs
   As with adults, there are wide variations both in what
adolescents believe and in the strength with which these
beliefs are held. In a national poll taken in the early 1950's
it was found that

> ...the typical American teenager today retains a favor-
> able attitude toward the church, attends services about
> once a week and says prayers once or twice a day...
> (He) thinks of God not as a person but as an omnipotent
> and omniscient bodiless spirit who exists everywhere
> ...He believes in the hereafter and expects his place
> there to be determined by his conduct here on earth.
> He believes that God guided or inspired the writing of
> the Bible, and that a good human society could not be
> built without such supernatural help (Remmers &
> Radler, 1957, pp. 155-6).

Although earlier studies had reached similar conclusions
(Kuhlen & Arnold, 1944; Ausubel, 1954), we cannot be sure

that such research findings accurately describe adolescent religion at present. In the previously mentioned study by Zuck and Getz (1968) it was found that a majority of the teenage respondants accepted the basic doctrines of their church without question, but this says little about teenagers in general since the researchers were only interested in the beliefs of those young people who were high school seniors and who were attending youth meetings in Evangelical Protestant churches. A much broader survey, conducted recently by Youth for Christ International, may give more information about the values and religious beliefs of youth, but the results are still being analyzed (Ward and Harmon, 1970). At present, it is probably more accurate to accept the conclusions of one report which, after reviewing a number of surveys conducted in the sixties, concluded that most teenagers now are "hedging"—showing neither a strong commitment nor a rejection of religious doctrines (Bealer & Willets, 1967). Stewart (1967) reached a similar conclusion after interviewing and analyzing the records of thirty young people who had been studied in a "normal development project" at the Menninger Foundation in Kansas. While most of these adolescents casually accepted the beliefs of their parents or church they had little real concern about religion or its influence in their lives.

Apparently, as they pass through the teenage years, most young people begin to question their beliefs. For many— one estimate places the figure at about two thirds of all adolescents (Landis, 1960)—there is *increased doubting*.

> The adolescent, as a part of his movement toward independence, feels constrained to examine and reconstruct the religious beliefs given him by his family. He may discard certain of the religious beliefs of childhood as he struggles in his search for his own set of values and his own identity. In order to become fully emancipated from his parents, it is usually necessary

for the adolescent to doubt the religious attitudes, standards, and value system of his parents. Involvement with and support from his peers involve the adolescent in a comparison of his religious beliefs with those of others. Such a comparison usually results in some change...(Knight, 1969, p.41).

While doubting may be present throughout adolescence, it is greatest around age seventeen. Girls doubt less than boys, adolescents in rural areas doubt less than those in the city, and those who have some denominational affiliation are less inclined to doubt than are those who have no such affiliation. It would appear that doubting is especially prevalent among the more intelligent, those in the higher socioeconomic groups, students in secular schools, those who have strong interests in science, teens who have "doubting friends," and those who have not had any firm religious training. Even when the training has been good, however, an adolescent is more inclined to doubt when he detects insincerity or bigotry in church leaders. "My father is a pillar in the church," one girl reported. "He is chairman of the deacon board, a Sunday school teacher, and involved in all kinds of church activities. But at home he is a tyrant—critical, and always hollering. He treats my mother like dirt. If that's what religion does, I want no part of it." When the sermons and youth programs seem to be irrelevant and when church leaders give pat answers and dogmatic pronouncements in response to teen questions, the young person is further inclined to doubt the church's message.

It should not be assumed that increased doubting is necessarily bad. John the Baptist doubted (Matthew 11:1-5) and so did Thomas (John 20:24-27). Instead of condemning them for doubting, Jesus provided the evidence that they needed in order to believe. As the adolescent moves into adulthood he may put away childish things including his immature conceptions of God, prayer, miracles, and the meaning of rituals. A reconsideration of earlier thinking in the light of later maturity, can produce a more healthy and biblically sound religious faith. The church, of course, should help the adolescent with this maturing process—answering his questions, discussing his doubts, showing him the evidence, and stimulating further deliberations. This is wiser than encouraging the teenager to remain a spiritual babe, to swallow dogmatic affirmations and to flounder as he tries to answer questions on his own.

All of this should not hide the fact that in addition to doubting, religious awakening or a *renewed interest* in religion is also a common adolescent occurrence. In late childhood, there was little concern for religious matters but during the teen years this changes. Many conversions occur during this period and because of this, denominational evangelistic programs and interdenominational organizations such as Youth for Christ or Young Life have been created to reach high schoolers for Christ. Teens who are involved in religious work are often zealous in their labors, enthusiastic in their evangelistic efforts, and firm in their defense of the faith. This is especially true when there are peers who share the same religious beliefs.

The spiritual awakening of adolescence may be due, in part, to the existence of teenage needs that can be met by religion. There is a need to find meaning and purpose in life; a need to find identity and a personal set of values; a need for security and "a very present help" in times of adolescent turmoil; and a need to confess one's faults, experience forgiveness, and know that there is another chance. A faith built on scriptural teachings can provide the basis for meeting these needs.

Adolescent Religious Behavior

In spite of the commonly observed *interest* in religion there is usually a decline in church *attendance* during adolescence. While this is due in part, to a let-up in parental pressure to attend, there is also a growing dissatisfaction with the church. In one survey a seminary professor (Hendricks, 1069) asked 800 teenagers why they had dropped out of the church. The five most common given reasons were as follows:

1. The Bible didn't touch our lives;
2. There was no provision for our social needs;
3. The church is not interested in our personal problems;
4. The church gave us no challenge or responsibility;
5. We saw inconsistency in adult lives.

Even those teenagers who continue to attend church become impatient with long irrelevant sermons, poorly taught Sunday school classes, and boring or poorly organized youth fellowships. There are so many other exciting things to occupy an adolescent's time that he doesn't react favorably or enthusiastically to "dead meetings," dictatorial leaders, or a dogmatic refusal to listen to the needs of teenagers. Those Protestant Evangelicals who remain in the church until their last year of high school, tend to be more satisfied with the church than other groups of teenagers but as the authors of this study acknowledge, this is a select group. The more dissatisfied young people have probably dropped out long before their senior high school year (Zuck & Getz, 1968).

Personal religious practices such as prayer and Bible study can also show a change during adolescence. Many conclude that prayer doesn't work so they abandon the practice.[3] Others limit their prayers to pray for deliverance in times of stress, while a few spend more or less regular periods of time in prayer and in reading Scripture or other religious materials. Teens who regularly pray and read the Bible have been compared with those who avoid such activities. It has been found that those who engage in these personal religious practices are more satisfied with themselves, less critical of the church, happier in their boy-girl relationships, and less inclined to doubt (Zuck & Getz, 1968). Of course, we cannot be sure whether private devotions cause or simply accompany these other characteristics.

Implications For Church Leaders

Almost without exception, those who work with adolescents in the church want to help these young people pass through the tumultuous teens. The conclusions listed in table 3-2 offer some practical advice that is worthy of consideration by any youth-leader, regardless of his theology. In addition to these suggestions, the church should be concerned with trying to understand the needs of teenagers and desirous of preparing them for the future.

Understanding Teens

Understanding starts with the church leadership. The pastor, and especially the youth workers, should make an attempt to learn what the teenagers are thinking. This learning can come through reading (it is for this reason that the present chapter has been written) but such reading *must* be supplemented with serious listening. Adults can always talk and dispense advice (and such activities are not, in themselves, bad) but often the advice is given too freely and too soon. It is important that we listen for a while first, and try to put ourselves in the place of the teenager. It would also help if we could listen to teenager's music since this reveals much about adolescent values and thinking. In these ways we might come to experience things from his point of view, develop a greater understanding of his thinking, and be much more effective as counselors.

The church leader can also encourage parents and church members to understand and listen to young people. On a number of occasions the author has used a technique which can increase understanding and open lines of communication.

97

Table 3—2

*Ways of Relating to Teens in the Church**

1. Encourage teens to read the Bible regularly and assist them in finding how to enjoy studying it and benefiting from it.

2. Help create in young people a greater confidence in witnessing to others about Christ and provide instruction in how to witness.

3. Give encouragement to Christian parents of teenagers in view of their rather significant influence on the lives of their children.

4. Instruct Christian parents on how to have meaningful family devotions with teens, how to discuss spiritual problems with their teens, and how to create a home atmosphere conducive to greater parent-teen rapport.

5. Minister to nonchristian parents, seeking to win them to Christ.

6. Enlist adult workers for youth who will make themselves available for personal counseling with teens, and train those workers how to counsel youth.

7. Plan church ministries for youth that will relate to their expressed needs for help (e.g., counsel on sexual problems, instruction on preparation for marriage, information on vocational opportunities, instruction on how to manage time and money, counsel on school problems).

8. Give opportunity for young people to discuss and find answers to their questions about biblical doctrines, particularly those teachings that appear irrational or seem to suggest incongruities within God's order of the universe.

9. Encourage adults in the church to be more consistent in living out the truths they profess to believe, and to show more genuine interest in an appreciation of the church's young people.

10. Raise the quality of Sunday school teaching in classes for the young people by injecting a greater variety of visual aids, encouraging more meaningful class discussion, and utilizing more captivating lesson introductions; and in youth programs, give more attention to careful planning of youth meetings and to selection of topics that will contribute to teens' Bible knowledge and spiritual growth.

11. Plan interchurch activities and other functions that will enable Christian teens to become acquainted with other Christian young people whom they may appropriately date.

12. Guide teens in finding the way to a more consistent Christian life, to an outworking of the moral standards which they profess.

13. Call attention to the fact that maintaining prolonged, close relationships in too frequent dating can increase one's moral problem.

14. Assist youth in thinking through reasons why the Bible forbids certain practices, thus helping teens transform external standards into internally personalized convictions.

15. Guide teens in discovering biblical principles for evaluating questionable practices not specifically prohibited by Scripture.

* From R.B. Zuck and G.A. Getz, *Christian Youth: An In-depth Study*. Chicago: Moody Press, 1968, p p. 161-162. Copyright ©National Sunday School Association. Used by permission.

In meetings on parent-teen relationships, everyone present is given a paper and invited to write (anonymously) an answer to the question "What is the biggest problem that you have in understanding teenagers (or parents." Parents put "P" at the top of their answer; teenagers put a "T." Then, while the group sings some hymns and makes announcements, these papers are sorted into categories of response. The papers are then read and both the leader and participants in the audience gave their reactions.

A similar procedure is very helpful in dealing with sex questions. Teenagers will write anonymous questions about sex that they would never have the courage to ask verbally from the floor. A husband and wife team, who are frank in their answers and not embarrassed to discuss sex in front of a group, can do much to impart accurate information and instill healthy sex attitudes.

Of course, lectures, reading, discussion groups, panel presentations, and other methods can all contribute to the greater understanding of teenagers (and other groups in the church).

Preparing for the Future

The church can play a significant role in preparing young people for the future. When they leave the security of their home churches and move to colleges, students often encounter a greater challenge to their faith than they ever experienced in high school. It is while they are still in high school, therefore, that teens must be given some preparation for the future. Psychological research would suggest the following practical guidelines for church youth leaders (Collins, 1963).

1. Warn teenagers that their beliefs will continue to be challenged and criticized. Most of them have experienced some of this in high school, but they are not prepared for the ridicule or thorny questions that will be raised by college professors and other students. Since high schoolers are not always receptive to advice from the "over-30 generation,"

it is often beneficial to have younger adults give a picture of what college will really be like, impart information, and work with the high schoolers.

2.   Instruct teens in their faith. The student who is not sure what he believes, or why, is a prime target for the doubt and confusion of the late teens and is of little value as a witness for Christ (I Peter 3:15).

3.   Teach what the non-Christian believes and why we disagree. Too often we don't bother to mention the arguments of the unbeliever and we wait, instead, until the teenager hears them on his own. This leaves the young Christian to fend for himself. Since he has never heard these issues in his home church, he concludes that Christians are "out of it" and unaware of the hard challenges to the faith. Sometimes this leads to bitterness and a decision to forget about religion. Surely it is better to raise these difficult issues when mature Christian counsel is available to help in their resolution. Youth workers, then should have at least some understanding of apologetics.

Summary

Adolescence is a period of transition during which an individual moves from the relative security of childhood to the privileges and responsibility of adulthood. In western society, this transition is often accompanied by confusion, turmoil, and frustration. The adolescent is no longer a child, but neither is he accepted as an adult. He grows to adult size and has sexual urges which are even more intense than those of most adults, but he must keep these impulses under control because he is denied the opportunity to marry and act as a sexually mature adult.

Adolescents are struggling for identity and independence of parental control. They want to be accepted by their peers, treated as adults by their parents, and respected by society. As they seek to find a purpose for living and a useful set of values, they engage in a variety of interests and develop idealistic aspirations for the future. Often they throw off immature views of religion and seek instead, for a more mature faith.

The church leader can seek to understand the thinking of these young people, listen to their problems, and prepare them for the future. Relevant, problem-centered, biblically based, carefully planned youth programs are essential for the church that would minister effectively to these young people.

Chapter Four

YOUNG ADULTHOOD: THE SETTLING YEARS

Young adulthood is usually defined as the years between the late teens and late thirties. During this period the individual "drops the pilot and starts sailing on his own." He has been taught to navigate, alerted to the changing currents, and warned of winds or dangerous reefs. Under supervision he has taken trips in sheltered waters and even done some sailing on his own. But now he assumes the privileges and responsibilities of launching out into the deep by himself. He must cope with the storms of life, unaided by the close supervision and guidance of past teachers. Often, he asks another to share the journey. Soon others join them, bidden or unbidden, and their welfare depends on the skills and stability of the captain and his copilot (Lidz, 1968).

During the twenty years of young adulthood, there is a shift from self-centered dependency to an independence that is alert to the welfare of others. At the height of his physical strength, the young adult's health is likely good, and his intellectual capabilities are keen. Concern about material possessions, status, and vocational achievement will be greater than previously. He will be actively involved in building a marriage, starting a family, acquiring a home, improving a community, making friends, building self-confidence, and "being a success." During his thirties, he will be more productive and achieve more than at any other time in his life (Hurlock, 1959; Lehman, 1953). He will have great energy, many interests, and a number of recreational activities.

He will also have problems. Situations will arise for which he has had no training. There will be goals that he cannot reach, failures that he did not anticipate, and frustrations that he would rather avoid. At times there may be loneliness, family problems, worry, financial strain, and the pressure of "making it" in a career or marriage.

Young adults must make decisions about four common issues. The first of these is higher education. The individual must decide whether or not to attend college and what to study. He must adjust to the demands of college life and, in the case of graduate students, accept the necessity of spending some of his best adult years in school. Secondly, there is the problem of the military. Should the elgible male enlist? How will time in the armed forces influence the serviceman, his girlfriend or his family? Thirdly, the young adult is concerned with selecting a mate and starting a family. Then, fourthly, there is the whole matter of one's career—choosing a vocation, finding a job, and getting established in the work.

These problems overlap considerably. The man who is starting a family is at the same time usually beginning a career; the college student may also be a housewife; and the serviceman, in spite of his military obligations, may be concerned nevertheless about finding a wife. In considering young adulthood, we should not lose sight of this overlap, but our discussion will be clearer if each of these issues is dealt with separately.

College Life

The pastor or other Christian worker who wants to minister to college students must know both the campus and the students (Kemp, 1967).

In North America, institutions of higher education are of five general types. *Liberal Arts Colleges* are typically small and often church related. The student at these schools has close contact with his professors and in some cases learns in an environment where the Bible is taken seriously and "Christlike" behavior is encouraged. While some liberal arts colleges, such as Carleton or Swarthmore, have good facilities, well-trained faculty and high academic standards, the majority are struggling to stay alive. Lacking the finances to construct good libraries, adequate buildings, properly equipped laboratories, and to pay decent faculty salaries (the national average is about $12,000) these schools often give a second rate education, but make exhorbitant claims about their quality and spirituality. *Commuter colleges* are usually state supported and in the student's own community. The schools are often small and instruction is usually good. Unfortunately, the student lives at home and misses most of the traditional college experiences. Tax supported *state colleges* often focus on vocational training although many offer both undergraduate and graduate degrees. Currently these institutions are growing rapidly in size, quality, and number. *Universities* are typically large. Since there is prestige in working for a university, since faculty salaries are high, and since facilities are usually good, these institutions are able to attract capable scholars to their faculties. But these professors must publish to survive! They consider research and scholarly writing to be of greatest importance, and have little interest in teaching. For graduate students who want to be specialists, this is a good environment. For undergraduates, education at a big university is likely to be poor (Woodring, 1968). *Professional schools* often stress good teaching, but their outlook can be narrow and too vocationally oriented. Teachers colleges, nursing schools, Bible institutes and some business colleges train high school graduates. Medical schools, seminaries, schools of social work, and similar institutions accept only students who have a well-rounded undergraduate education.[1]

These institutions differ in size, quality, admission policies, curricula and spiritual concern. All are run by administrators —usually a president and deans—who must answer to the demands of a board of trustees, accrediting agencies, a constituency that often controls the purse strings, alumni, faculty, students, and the peering eyes of other institutions. The faculty are hired to teach, encouraged (and in many cases pressured) to publish, and expected to advise students, participate on committees, take part in professional activities, and serve the community. The staff, which includes secretaries, janitors, maintenance men, and dorm mothers, keep the institution running in its day-to-day activities. Then there are the students—roughly seven million of them in North America.

Robert Frost is said to have once commented that we put helpless old people in hospitals and helpless young people in college. While few students are actually helpless, many are surprised and almost overwhelmed by the pressures of the campus. Intense academic competition, impersonal registration procedures, teachers who can't communicate, homesickness, inconsiderate roommates and institutional food can all be very trying. Confusion results when respected professors criticize the student's religious or moral views. Great anxiety exists for students who maintained good grades in high school and suddenly find themselves in a struggle to survive academically. Many discover that their reading and study skills are poor or that they lack the self-discipline to study when no one is around to encourage them to "hit the books." Indeed, the whole issue of a newly-felt independence can be a problem. No one urges him to attend church. No adult reminds him that long coffee breaks, frequent dating, and late dormitory bull sessions may all contribute to lower grades. Finally, there is the influence of new standards of behavior. Young adults want to be accepted—especially when they are in the loneliness of an impersonal campus. But the price of acceptance is often participation in activities which the student has always considered wrong. Older students are often willing to "take a chance" on cheating, sexual promiscuity, drinking, or experimenting with drugs. They are gambling that these activities will bring them a thrill and not adversely influence their later career (Eddy, 1959). Younger students see this and must decide if they too are going to engage in such activities.

Colleges and universities have recently been the scenes of much student unrest. In analyzing this behavior, we might liken college-age youth to the passengers on a sinking ship. Some ignore the whole situation and continue playing bridge in the lounge; others rush around plugging up holes, bailing out water, and trying to keep the vessel afloat; the rest panic, assume the worst, take to the lifeboats and leave the ship (Pike, 1967). The *majority* of contemporary students are attending classes, reading textbooks, writing papers and dutifully meeting the standards of an institution which will, in time, award a diploma that is a stepping stone to higher status and bigger pay checks. A second group—known as the activists, or "young radicals" (Keniston, 1968)—have become concerned about the world's evils, and impatient with the seeming lack of concern and inactivity of the older generation or "Establishment." In encouraging protest, one college senior wrote,

> Any student who can sit through four years of college without once getting excited enough about the war in Viet-Nam or Communism in Cuba, voting discrimination in the South or the plight of the Jews in Russia to investigate the problem (study) and find others who agree with him and make some public protest—any student so dense or just plain selfish that he has not perceived the relation between his university education and the pressing questions of his society has undoubtedly been wasting his time (Gonzales, 1966, p. 112).

The student activist wants to alter the status quo. The laws of the land give him the right to speak his mind, and so he protests against suffering and injustice. He works to change

107

the plight of the oppressed and to teach the uneducated. He believes that resistance and civil disobedience may be courageous, justified, and the best way to bring about change (Resist, 1968). Often, in his enthusiasm, he is also guilty of oppressing and denying the rights of those with whom he disagrees. A third broad grouping of students are the alienated. Like the *activists,* these people are dissatisfied with the ills of society. But instead of rebelling or trying to change things, the alienated more often turn their backs on the "establishment" and "drop out," often with the aid of drugs. Their dress, moral standards, voluntary poverty, and blase manner of living are in sharp contrast to the striving and status seeking of the rest of society. Many, perhaps most, of these people become disinterested in the requirements of struggling for a college degree, so they leave school and live in hippie communities or with other alienated young adults (Kanter, 1970).[2]

There is no such thing as a "typical college student." But there are typical college student problems which are faced by many young adults as they pass through institutions of higher learning. There is a struggle to keep up in the midst of intense academic pressures; a desire to be accepted by one's peers; a striving for independence which is blocked by all kinds of college rules and regulations; a search for values and standards to guide one's behavior; frustration concerning an unknown future and a rapidly changing world; a struggle to find identity, purpose and meaning in life; concern about the world's evils (a concern that is accentuated by "on the spot" reports from the mass media); and disgust with an educational system that is characterized by boring irrelevant courses, disinterested professors, and narrow overspecialization.

Student Religion

Where is God in the midst of this? According to religious surveys, most students believe in God, but few have a dynamic faith which makes any real difference in their lives. Church attendance drops during the college years, and interest in spiritual things wanes. When considering religion, most students would probably accept one or more of the following views (Walsh, 1962; Bonnell, 1964; Novak, 1961).

1. "I'm tired of religion with its narrow rules and boring rituals." Many students criticize church goers for being hypocritical, denominationally narrow, rigid, and afraid to have any fun. Christians are rejected because they "live by blind faith and are afraid to look real facts in the face" (Walsh, 1962, p. 99). Great numbers of students are reacting against what they see as the naivete and irrelevance of their early religious upbringing.

2. "It doesn't matter what you believe as long as you're sincere." Students show tolerance for different religious views and often embrace a relativism which says that no religion is completely true. All beliefs have some good points, this position holds, it all depends on how you look at it. This philosophy is intolerant of people who try to convert students to a particular religious system.

3. "Religion is a crutch for weak people." This view stems from Marx and Freud. It reflects an incomplete view of religion, including Christianity. The Christian faith is not solely padding that one uses to keep from getting bruised. It is a relationship with a Person, and a way of life which offers challenge and frustrations—as well as help in time of need.

4. "Religion is old fashioned and irrelevant." Students are more interested in social involvement, science, progress, "turning on" with drugs, and "living it up." These gods are more attractive than the God of Abraham, Isaac and Jacob.

5. "Religion just doesn't make sense." People who consider themselves to be intellectually sophisticated have trouble accepting the authority of the Bible or the virgin birth, divinity, resurrection and (for some) even the his-

torical existence of Christ. For many, the question of how a loving God could tolerate evil in the world is a stumbling block. The Bible, of course predicted that its message would not make sense to nonbelievers (I Corinthians 2:14; 1:18, 23).

6. "I'm not willing to commit myself to God." The same people who accept by faith the presuppositions of science, who commit themselves to the power of some drug, or who search for meaning in life, are unwilling to yield to Christ.

Implications for Church Leaders

There are perhaps few mission fields today as open, as ripe for harvest, or as difficult to reach as the modern college campus. In meeting the needs of contemporary students the church leader might consider the following:

1. Stimulate understanding in the congregation. Too many church members, especially those who are not college graduates, have a distorted view of the campus today. There is little appreciation for the intense pressures on students and little tolerance for their behavior. The church (and the religious leader) that is concerned about the campus must know something about the campus.

2. Be concerned about relevance and intellectual matters. This is not a plea to forsake the truths of Scripture or to ignore "the faith which was once delivered unto the saints" (Jude 3). On the contrary, it is a challenge for the church to defend the faith (Phil. 1:17 b, Titus 1:13 b, Jude 3), and to show its modern relevance to the needs of men. "For decades there have been too few men, at once intellectual and religious and wise on the campuses.... The churches are filled with worshipers but intelligence has fled the ranks" (Novak, 1961, p. 178). We need more men like C. S. Lewis who can present the truths of Christianity to thinking intellectuals. We need competent professors who are not silent and ashamed of their Christian beliefs. We need college programs in the churches which face the intellectual and other problems of students, dealing with them in a

110

straightforward manner. The churches must show students that the gospel of Christ provides intellectual challenge, social concern, and practical relevance.

3. Provide guidance, counseling, and pastoral care for students. For campus churches, or for those near a campus, direct contact with students will be an important part of the church's ministry. For other congregations a ministry of preparing people for college may be more important and more practical.

In either situation, guidance, counseling and pastoral care are important. *Guidance* refers to giving information and helping students as they make decisions and formulate plans. *Counseling* is more concerned with feelings such as doubt, inadequacy, guilt, hostility, meaninglessness, frustration, and unworthiness. *Pastoral care* involves support and encouragement in times of sickness, trouble, sorrow, or other need (Kemp, 1967).

4. Seek to win students to Christ. Organizations such as Inter-Varsity Christian Fellowship or Campus Crusade for Christ have discovered a great spiritual hunger among contemporary collegians. Christians should support such efforts, cooperate with them, and—where geographically possible—become actively involved in campus evangelism.

In contacts with college students it is wise to remember their problems, their working-environment, and some of their criticisms of the church. Young intellectuals will often buy "the old, old story of Jesus and His love," but they have no time for the rigidity, squabbling, and man-made traditions of many churches. There is no need to change our message. It's relevance is timeless. But in reaching students we might look again at some of our attitudes and long established ways of doing things.

The Military

In some respects, life in the armed forces is similar to life in college. There is loneliness, excessive pressure, study

111

demands, institutional food, inconsiderate "roommates," and peer group encouragement to engage in behavior which the serviceman might prefer to avoid. In addition, there are all the typical pressures of young adulthood—finding one's identity, choosing a mate, experiencing independence —problems which do not disappear just because someone puts on a uniform.

But the military is also unique. The young serviceman must undergo the physical and psychological stresses of boot camp; he must learn to accept authority and to obey without question; he must be neat, well-groomed, and prompt; he must endure boredom, monotony and loneliness, with little chance to escape or change his routine; his sexual urges must somehow be kept under control; and he must live on a low salary with no opportunities to supplement his income. Then there are the problems of separation. Disagreements with family, concern about the faithfulness of a girlfriend, separation from children, or the insecurity of knowing that "my wife seems to get along pretty well without me" (and, by implication, "may no longer need me") —these and other problems are accentuated by distance and the necessity of communicating by letters.

Of course, military experiences are not all bad. The Armed Services teach self-discipline and respect for author-ity. In addition the chance to travel, the educational opportunities, and the fellowship with friends can all be very desirable. But recruiters tell only part of the story and movies make the military look much more glamorous than it really is. It is nice to be admired when your mother or girlfriend first sees you in uniform, but this does little to offset the pressures of service life.

In war times these difficulties are especially intense. Most men in combat are young, away from home, in foreign surroundings, and living under conditions that are far from comfortable. There is great physical danger, continual observation of death and suffering, and the necessity to kill

—even when this leads to feelings of guilt. It is not surprising that many men are scared, but feel social pressures to do their job without letting down their buddies.

Although dedicated chaplains minister to men and women in uniform and conduct regular services in military chapels, there is little widespread interest in Christianity among the troops. Contrary to popular opinion, even battle experience does not lead to increased interest in religion. It was discovered in one study that only twenty-six per cent of the veterans interviewed claimed to be more religious following military experience, nineteen per cent were less religious, and fifty-five per cent said that war made them neither more nor less religious (Allport, 1951). In spite of this general lack of spiritual concern, organizations such as the Officers' Christian Union and the Enlisted Men's Christian Union exist to stimulate prayer and Bible study among military personnel. In addition, there are individuals and small groups of believers in all branches of the service who are vitally interested in spiritual matters and who meet together informally when time and circumstances permit.

We must also remember that for some young adults, problems with the military come long before they ever don a uniform or take an oath of allegiance. These men frequently experience fear of the draft, a struggle over the morality of war, and an unwillingness to "risk separation from their families and their country, destruction of their careers, loss of their freedom and loss of their lives" (Leinwans, 1968, p. 100; Whitlock, 1968).

Implications for Church Leaders

The local church and its leaders can minister to servicemen in four distinct ways. These could be labeled "understanding," "preparation," "keeping in touch," and "helping with readjustment."

1. Understanding. When members of the local church have some understanding of service conditions, they can

better appreciate the serviceman, his family, and his problems. Discussions with returned servicemen, or a visit with a chaplain can reveal a great deal about contemporary military life.

2. Preparation. Churches today recognize the importance of preparing people for dating, college and the selection of a mate, but we should also be doing something for those who are facing military service. One chaplain (Harris, 1966) has suggested that one or more churches might plan a series of lectures and discussions about military life. These could be led by veterans, local recruiters, or nearby chaplains. While such a program would be valuable, we must do more than impart facts. In private conferences or small groups, the future serviceman should have opportunity to face his fears, discuss his conflicts, consider his feelings about war, and talk about his spiritual development in the service.

3. Keeping in Touch. "It is important that the local church follow its members through the mails—not as a patronizing gesture...but as an honest expression of continuing concern.... Nothing can take the place of the knowledge that 'your home church misses you'" and is praying for you (Harris, 1966, pp. 108-9). In addition to writing letters, church leaders can keep the congregation aware of the location and activity of members in the service. Some churches publicly acknowledge the serviceman's departure and welcome him when he returns home. Sometimes pictures are displayed in the lobby, portions of letters are published in the church paper, and there is a "serviceman of the week" whose name is printed in the bulletin and mentioned in the pastoral prayer on Sunday.

4. Helping with Readjustment. Although the days to the "end of the stretch" may have been counted and eagerly marked off on a calendar, readjustment to civilian life is not always easy. The ways of the military are often hard to shake off when it comes time to hang up the uniform. The

church leader can provide understanding, support, and helpful counsel to the veteran and his family during the weeks of readjustment to civilian life.

Starting A Family

There are a number of reasons why people marry. The most obvious are a desire for love and companionship, a need for sexual intimacy, and a desire to be parents. [3] Less logical reasons include a seeking for adventure, a wish to get away from home, a chance to enhance one's social status, or a desire to escape from the stigma of being an "old maid" or "bachelor."

Getting married and starting a family involves at least five major hurdles. First one must find a mate. Then, a couple must learn to live together, develop an ability to handle money, adjust sexually, and meet the realities of parenthood.

In selecting a mate, people usually choose someone of similar race, religion, education, intelligence, social class, age (although many agree that the man should be a little older), previous marital status (divorced people, for example, usually marry other divorced people,) attitudes, values, and desired number of children (Berelson and Steiner, 1964). There is also a tendency for people with similar personality characteristics to marry—although at least some variation is desirable.

To find a mate, young adults must get into situations where there is opportunity to meet and date a variety of eligibles. There must be a willingness both to date the same person several times, and when appropriate, to become deeply involved emotionally. For some people, this is very difficult. Afraid that they might not be accepted if they are really known, these people are too insecure to develop a close relationship with a member of the opposite sex. They may date the same person several times, but they avoid any serious involvements. It is a lot safer, they believe, to keep the opposite sex at a distance, both psychologically and physically. Even when a couple has decided to get married there is often anxiety as they contemplate the responsibilities and consequences of being committed to and closely dependent upon another person.

After they say "I do" a husband and wife must learn to live together. At first this is easy. The couple is intrigued with their new status and happy with the sexual freedom of marriage. Very soon, however, demanding adjustment problems arise. The intimacy of living together leads to a more realistic mutual appraisal. Mannerisms, temperamental ways, expectations, habits, and attitudes that might have been hidden or overlooked during courtship are revealed and this sometimes leads to irritation and friction. There must be a new way of living, a change in one's social activities, and a learning to think in the plural ("ours") instead of in the singular ("mine"). When there are disagreements, the couple must discover that refusing to speak, arguing, or meekly giving in for the sake of peace, are all temporary and unsatisfactory solutions. There must be, instead, a mutual adaptation in which each seeks to understand and appreciate the other's point of view (Hurlock, 1959). This involves communication of thoughts, attitudes, or feelings and a desire to work together in solving problems.

For some couples, learning to live together is much easier than for others. Surveys have shown that husbands and wives are better able to adjust when they have come from happy homes; have had good relationships with their parents; have been disciplined as children—firmly but not harshly; have grown up in a situation where sex is discussed openly; have known each other for more than six months; are out of the teens at the time of marriage; have some college education; and attend church together on a regular basis (Terman, 1938; Burgess, Locke and Thomas, 1963). Even when, as in most cases, all of these desired conditions

116

do not exist, determined couples can work together to insure the success of a marriage. The rewards of real marital happiness make the effort worthwhile.

Finances can be a major issue for the young husband and wife. If both work during their early years together, there is often a more substantial income which permits them to get the things they want. When there can be economic security in the form of savings, absence of debt, and no need to borrow, there is better marital adjustment. But what if money is scarce or the couple disagrees on the ways in which finances are to be handled? The married couple must learn to budget, to make decisions about joint checking accounts, to decide who pays the bills, and to reach agreement on what they need as opposed to what they might want but cannot afford. Problems arise when there is disagreement over these matters or when there are conflicting opinions concerning the use of charge accounts, the wisdom of installment buying, the need for budgeting or the distribution of joint earnings.

Problems in *sexual adjustment* often come early in marriage. Frequently, a couple approaches their wedding night with high expectations. But when inexperience, ignorance, embarrassment and difficulties in communication interfere with intercourse, there can be frustration and disappointment. The married couple may have an abundance of information about sex, but their attitudes or past experiences can interfere with successful sexual adjustment. Such physical incompatibility is often blamed as a cause of marital difficulties, but it may be more accurate to conclude that the reverse is true. Sexual difficulties are created or accentuated when there are other problems in the marriage. When these other problems are ironed out, the sex problems often disappear also.

When the time comes to start a family, *parenthood* may be approached with mixed feelings. While most want children, few parents are prepared for the accompanying loss of freedom, financial sacrifices, or demands on one's time and energy. Sometimes, parents and prospective parents wish that there were no children around or expected. These feelings, while common at times, often produce a sense of guilt in the young mother or father. When the child finally arrives, there is frequently an almost overwhelming sense of responsibility, coupled with feelings of inadequacy and a desire to "do the right thing."

Implications for Church Leaders

The Bible makes a number of statements about husband-wife relationships and child rearing. Any church which is concerned about biblical teaching and the needs of church members, must not overlook the responsibility of stimulating good family life. This can be done in sermons, Bible study classes, or personal counseling. There is also great value in discussion groups for newlyweds or young parents (Ellzey, 1968). When couples get together to discuss the problems of young married life or parenthood, there can be mutual support and a helpful sharing of information.

Several years ago, one church began a club for young mothers who met monthly to share their concerns, their problems, and the knowledge about child rearing that they had gleaned from reading or discussions with others. The club was so enthusiastically received that fathers became involved and the group (plus others which started later) continued until the participants became grandparents (Bell and Bell, 1968). In addition to helping the parents, such programs can also stimulate spiritual development, both in the group members and in their children.

The Single Adult

With the emphasis that our society puts on marriage and the family, it is easy to forget that some people are unattached. These people — including the unmarried, the

118

widowed, and the divorced — are probably the most neglected group in the church. There are programs for children, teenagers, college students, and married couples, but very few churches have a place for single adults. These people are more often forgotten or passed off as impulsive, unreliable, and perhaps even unspiritual misfits. Professor Elmer Towns has succinctly and humorously described the frustrations of single adults:

> If you are single and under thirty-five, don't try a church for friendship and meeting a mate. . . .The church on the corner with its steeple pointing to God and its stained glass windows shutting out the world shouts to the careerist: 'Stay away.' . . .Of course there are high school classes with pimply-faced boys flirting with giggly girls. An usher may have tried to deposit you there, but that is an insult because you're an adult.
>
> Or he might have taken you to the adult class entitled, 'Homebuilders.' The name has a matrimonial ring and just rubs salt in your 'single' sores.
>
> 'Not for me,' replied an assistant editor who was invited to a 'homebuilders' class. 'Observing the love and companionship of a married couple leaves me lonelier than ever, or some jealous wife claims I'm after her husband.'
>
> The sermon is many times the crowning insult. Salvation is pictured as marriage. Christ is pictured as the Bridegroom, and the repentant sinner as the bride. But you want the real thing: a human relationship with someone who understands you.
>
> And if you're searching for fellowship, watch out for those church socials. While men play softball or discuss the Green Bay Packers, you'll sit with the wives and learn about Johnny's two new teeth or how to make a budget-stretching souffle.

Most single careerists avoid getting involved. If they seriously want to learn about God, they sneak into church on Sunday morning, worship God and escape after the service with a minimum of damage to their self-respect.

So you're determined to be an active member? Stay in church two years and see if they elect you to any position. Some elder is sure to find the place in Scripture that names the qualifications for the official board: 'Husband of one wife. . . .' And you are single.

If you are a woman, they may let you teach in the Sunday school. It saves them the trouble of finding you a suitable class. . . .

The average church is, above all, conservative. They think of you as fast, flighty and free, but won't say it to your face. As one elder said, 'You can't build a mature congregation on single people' (Towns, 1968, pp. 18-19).

Many unmarried people want to marry, but have not had the opportunity. Because of their personality characteristics, physical features, or a shortage of eligible partners, such persons have never found a mate. It should not be assumed, however, that all unmarried people are dissatisfied with their situation. Some prefer to remain unattached. They may be more concerned with their careers or independence. Some "just haven't found the right person." Others think marriage is too risky or unpleasant. A few, including the apostle Paul (I Corinthians 7:8, 32) may prefer to avoid marriage, so they can devote themselves to Christian service (Towns, 1967).

The unmarried and formerly married have a number of unique adjustment problems. These include the following.

The Search for a New Identity
The single adult must face the prospect that he or she may never marry. This is a bitter pill for many to swallow,

especially in view of society's unkind and critical attitudes toward the unmarried. Some refuse to accept this fact and scramble frantically to find a spouse. Others feel self-pity and inferiority. All must adjust to the realities of life without a mate (Towns, 1967).

Coupled with the search for identity is the search for meaning in life. The happily married person shares his ambitions and frustrations with his spouse; both the husband and wife work to improve their situation as a family. But why does a single person strive? Who cares about his (or her) achievements? Part of the search for a new identity involves finding meaning for a life that is lived alone.

Loneliness

The unmarried have independence, material possessions, and the opportunity to travel. But there can also be great loneliness, a longing for close human companionship and a desire to be needed. One writer has suggested that most, if not all of the problems of the unmarried can be traced to their isolation (Hugen, 1959). This is accentuated if the person lives away from his family. Thanksgiving, Christmas, birthdays, and other family times can become especially lonely. A close relationship with God and an awareness of being loved by Him, can be powerful antidotes to loneliness, but human companionship is also needed. Adam was in close contact with God, but the Lord made a human companion because "it is not good" for a human being to be alone (Genesis 2:18).

Part of the feeling of isolation comes because the single adult has difficulty finding acceptance in the community. He pays higher insurance rates, has a lower credit rating, and often has difficulty getting a good job—all because people think that the unmarried are less stable.

Sex

Inherent in singleness is the problem of handling the sex drive. Paul warned that this could be a great stress

121

(I Corinthians 7:8-9). When there is little hope of achieving a sexual union in marriage, the single person is sometimes tempted to engage in illicit affairs of a heterosexual or homosexual nature. The temptation is greater if it offers even temporary intimacy and acceptance for lonely people.

There are no simple answers to this sex problem. Undoubtedly the Christian relies on the Holy Spirit to give self-control, but even when controlled, the drive still persists.

Implications for Church Leaders

"Long ago I learned that the churches are for the old and the young and for cozy little families," commented one single woman. "Without knowing love, or feeling any sense of grace to uphold you, it is not easy to believe that God loves you, or that he wishes to prepare you for some service. . . .You want reassurance that you're heard and wanted" (Payne, 1968, p. 45). It is easy to forget that during His adult life, Jesus was in the unmarried category Himself. When He called the "heavy laden" (Matthew 11:28), He surely included those who were single. Likewise, the church cannot ignore such an important segment of our society.

At least two practical steps can be taken in ministering to the unmarried. First, we can *develop an understanding and concern.* When we know something about the normal adjustments of living alone, we are more inclined to be concerned about young adults, and less inclined to pass them off as irresponsible misfits. As the church better understands the single adult, it is better able to minister to him (Towns, 1967).

Secondly, we can attempt to *meet the needs* of the young adult. Here is a field for evangelism. The unmarried needs to experience the love of God and the abundant life that comes to the followers of Christ (John 10:10). He needs a place where there is fellowship both with families and with others of similar age and status. He needs people who can give counsel and acceptance. He needs a program that is Bible centered and geared to practical needs. Such programs must involve lively social events, discussions of relevant topics, and opportunities for service. Finally, there is a need for responsibility. The unmarried have no family obligations to tie them down. They are free to be actively involved in church activities—and when given responsibilities, they can be among the most faithful and productive workers in the church. This should come as no surprise. Paul reached the same conclusion many centuries ago (I Corinthians 7:32-34).

Launching a Career

When a person chooses an occupation, he is also choosing a way of life. His status in the community, his circle of friends, his leisure activities, his values, his interests, his goals in life, and to some extent his personality development and the future of his children are all related to his occupation. If a man (or woman) is unhappy with his work, he is also likely to be unhappy with life in general.

In terms of vocational development, the individual in the late teens and early twenties is in "exploration stage." This involves self-examination and looking around for a suitable kind of work. There may be a shift from job to job or a changing of majors in college. Often there are unrealistically high aspirations that must be lowered to meet one's capacities.

From the mid-twenties until the early forties, there is a move into the "establishment stage." The person has chosen some line of work and is attempting to move ahead and succeed in his field (Arkoff, 1968). As indicated earlier in the chapter, his most productive years of vocational achievements will probably come during the thirties (Lehman, 1953).

But not all people are happy in their work. Many have "fallen into" a job without much training or forethought and this often leads to unhappiness and dissatisfaction. In general, those who have been able to select a vocation on the basis of their abilities and interests, are much more satisfied (Lipsitt and Wilson, 1954).

Does the problem of one's work and career have any implications for the church? The answer is clearly "yes." In Ephesians 6, Paul indicated that the employee should work as if Christ were his boss. The Christian must recognize that God calls some to be preachers, and some to be teachers. But He also wants truck drivers, housewives, secretaries, and physicians to serve Him through their particular vocations. There is no biblical heirarchy with missionaries at the top spiritually, pastors next, and others somewhere below. All believers are expected to serve faithfully in their various occupations as good soldiers of Christ. These truths should be emphasized in the local church.

The church leader and his congregation should also realize that many people have difficulty settling on an occupation and that many (including full-time church workers) sometimes feel led to change vocations. The church should provide vocational counseling for the young and the dissatisfied; encouragement for the frustrated; and alternate opportunities for those who have found little enjoyment out of their work.

Religion in Young Adulthood

By the time the individual reaches adulthood, either he has resolved his religious doubts and formulated a philosophy of life, based on religion, that will be satisfactory to him, with minor changes, for the rest of his life, or he has rejected religion as having little or nothing to offer him. In both cases, religion has less interest for the individual than it had when he was younger. The early twenties have been called the 'least religious period of life' (Hurlock, 1959, p. 392).

This is a time when participation in religious services drops (Kuhlen, 1962). God is no longer seen as a personal being who loves and protects men (McCann, 1955), interest in religion has declined, and the individual is more concerned about other matters. It has been shown that those who participate in religious observances show better personal and social adjustment than those who avoid religion, but this does not mean that religion is causing better adjustment. The reverse may also be true: more stable adults maintain an interest in spiritual matters (Moberg, 1968).

When the responsibilities of parenthood are assumed, interest in religion begins to revive. Parents want their children to get religious training and frequently the whole family returns to church (Hurlock, 1959). During the thirties, therefore, church attendance increases and by the forties it is at the highest adult level (Moberg, 1968).

Many churches find that they have a large number of children and adolescents, many people in middle and old age, but few young couples. To remedy this situation, and fill the "young adult gap," church members must make the effort to go out, find young adults, and encourage them to come in. But the church programs must be relevant and geared to human needs. Otherwise, young adults if they come, are not likely to stay.

Summary

In the years between the late teens and late thirties, the individual moves out from under the parental umbrella and begins life on his own. For many, there is further training in colleges. Others must face a military obligation. Almost all are concerned about finding a mate and beginning a career.

In the midst of these responsibilities and ambitions, there is often a loss of interest in religion. Church attendance drops and spiritual matters are forgotten. Sometimes the church, in turn, forgets the young adult. But we have a responsibility for this segment of society and we must be concerned about evangelizing, training, counseling, and providing fellowship for young adults and all other age groups in the church.

Chapter Five

MIDDLE AND OLD AGE: THE MATURE YEARS

According to the old saying, "Life begins at forty." As they move into middle age, most people are still active, vigorous, and alert. Finding one's identity or purpose in life is no longer a great problem. The individual is established in his work, and is about to enter the period of his greatest earning capacity and the peak of his authority and prestige. With their children nearly grown up, parents are being released from the responsibilities of constant protection and supervision. A new interest and involvement in social, community, and church affairs is developing. The adult is moving into what Jung has called "a time of supreme psychological importance. . .the afternoon of life" when the second half of our earthly pilgrimage begins (1961, p. 119-122).

Like other periods of life, the middle years, and old age which follows, are not free of problems. Our western society places great emphasis on youth, and as people grow older, they are likely to feel less and less wanted. With middle age, the individual begins to realize that he has passed the half-way point in his life. He recognizes that physical attractiveness and mental capacities are already starting to decline. Often there is a re-evaluation of his life goals, and a contemplation of what can be accomplished in the time that remains.

For many years, psychologists and other scientists focused their attention on the characteristics and problems of the young, but middle and old age were largely ignored. Happily, this situation has now begun to change. Many investigators have developed a concern about the nature of old age and, more recently, there has been an upsurge of interest in the middle years.

127

Like the rest of society, the church has also ignored its older members. As indicated in the previous chapter, church attendance is highest during the forties and early fifties. The middle aged adult contributes more to the church than any other age group. The church leadership is likely to be middle aged and many of the most active members are over forty. But the unique problems and characteristics of adulthood are often overlooked. Undoubtedly, most church leaders could profit from a fresh look at adulthood, and from a re-evaluation of the church's ministry to those who are in the "over forty generation."

Middle Age

Middle age is usually defined as the years between forty and the early sixties. Unlike earlier periods in life when there is some specific body change, there are no abrupt physical events to herald middle age. The move from young adulthood to middle life involves, instead, the passage of time and a changing state of mind. The individual becomes aware that his body is slowing down. He realizes that his children are growing into adulthood and that the peak years of his life are passing. He often takes stock of his life thus far and seeks to re-evaluate his future goals (Lidz, 1968).

Of course, there are great individual differences in how one reacts to middle age. Many people accept it and push on to reach the peak of achievement in their careers. As family responsibilities decrease and one's economic status improves, there is often a renewed interest in socializing—especially with a few close friends. For many, there is greater involvement in community affairs and a new interest in hobbies. Physically demanding activities are avoided, but there is an upsurge of reading, watching television, and participation in similar non-strenuous activities. Although there is no evidence that middle age brings new interests, it appears that the things people liked most at twenty-five years of age are liked even more with increasing age, and the things liked least at twenty-five are liked less and less. This is especially true of one's reactions to people and amusements, and of the opinions that individuals have about themselves (Strong, 1963).

Of course, there are some people who refuse to accept the fact that they are growing older. Many feel threatened by the ambitions of a younger generation. Instead of realizing that added satisfactions are available as one matures, these people dress and act like young people—and cling to their children. Carl Jung, the famous Swiss psychiatrist described this concisely:

> Man has two aims: The first is the . . . begetting of children and all the business of protecting the brood; to this period belongs the gaining of money and social position. When this aim is satisfied, there begins another phase, namely, that of culture (the concern with the wider world around us and the meaning of life). For the attainment of the former goal we have the help of nature, and moreover of education; but little or nothing helps us toward the latter goal. Indeed, often a false ambition survives, in that an old man wants to be a youth again, or at least feels he must behave like one, although within himself he can no longer make believe. . . .Many people. . .cling to the illusions of youth, or at least to their children, in order to preserve in this way a fragment of illusion. One sees this in mothers, who find in their children their only justification, and who imagine they have to sink away into empty nothingness when they give them up. It is no wonder, then, that many bad neuroses develop at the beginning of the afternoon of life. It is a kind of second puberty period, a like repetition of storm and stress, not infrequently accompanied by all the tempests of passion (1961, p. 125).

Whether or not this will be a period of storm and stress depends on how one reacts to the three major issues of middle age: physical changes, family changes, and vocational problems (Hurlock, 1959). Let us consider each of these in turn.

Physical Changes

In middle age, one must adjust to slowly developing changes in one's appearance, physical abilities, and health. Flabby skin, a few wrinkles, a greying or thinning of the hair, and a "middle aged spread" or "spare tire" around the waistline are tell-tale signs of middle age.

Although the individual may be reluctant to admit it, middle age also brings a gradual decline in physical skills and abilities. Hearing becomes slightly impaired and vision deteriorates—often making bifocals necessary. Reaction time is a little slower, muscles lose some resiliency, bones become a little more brittle, and the digestive process slows down—often leading to problems with constipation. Intellectual functioning also becomes a little less efficient, especially if one is not actively involved in using one's mental capacities. The middle-aged person who returns to school after a long absence may find that study and memorizing are more difficult than before.

During the forties and fifties, there is a general decline in physical fitness and some deterioration in health (Hurlock, 1959). Men become more susceptible to heart attacks and malignancies take their toll in women. Many middle-age health problems can be avoided by frequent and regular medical checkups, but the healthy person often continues driving himself, ignoring his physical condition. Not until an unexpected illness forces him to slow down will he take better care of himself. One writer has suggested that a good way to assure long life is for a man to suffer a mild heart attack in middle age. This usually causes him to slow down, "take it easy," and keep an eye on his health (Litz, 1968).

130

Many of these physical changes are not nearly as bad as the psychological impact that they have on the individual. Grey hair, for example, or a receeding hairline are visible indications of age. Some people feel very self conscious about changes such as these. Hair dyes, toupees, skin creams, body-building courses, and similar devices are used in an attempt to hide — often from oneself — the evidences of aging. Some men become concerned about a loss of virility, and it is not uncommon for them to chase after young girls in an attempt to convince themselves that they are still sexually attractive. Others continue to engage in strenuous physical feats, just to prove to themselves or others that they are still "able to take it." Often, these people find that they are not as attractive or as strong as they once were, and sometimes they are forced to the abrupt recognition that they really are getting older.

The most pronounced physical and psychological changes of middle age are undoubtedly those that relate to sexual functioning. This is especially true in women. During the late forties, most women experience the *menopause* or "change of life." This involves a slowing down of the menstrual flow until it eventually stops and the woman's potential for child bearing has ended. For many women menopause is a time of psychological stress and physical discomfort. Nervous tension, irritability, depression, insomnia, waves of hot-feelings known as "hot flashes," unexpected sweating, dizziness, headaches, and itching or tingling of the skin are common symptoms (Lewis & Gilmore, 1965). While many of these are the result of changes in hormone secretions, much of the discomfort of the menopause is psychologically caused. Old wives tales lead many to believe that this is a time of serious emotional and mental instability accompanied by extreme physical pain (Litz, 1968). In one study of middle aged women, fifty-eight per cent agreed that the menopause is unpleasant; fifty-nine per cent said women should expect trouble during this time; fifty-seven per cent said women dread this, and; fifty-three per cent believed that in menopause, a woman is apt to do "crazy things" (Neugarten, 1967). Some feel that the loss of one's child-bearing ability ends one's enjoyment of intercourse and leads to a loss of femininity. It appears, however, that many of these fears are overemphasized and even untrue. The physical discomforts can be largely removed by the injection of hormones. The ability to experience sexual satisfactions usually remains the same and often increases. But even when a woman experiences no phychological stress herself, she concludes that she is an exception and continues to believe the folklore that surrounds the menopause.

The male *climacteric* is a loss of reproductive powers that usually occurs in the sixties or seventies and is much slower than the female menopause. Most males do not experience physical and psychological sysptoms at this time, although there is evidence to suggest that some men, like women, experience a "change in life," with accompanying nervousness, hot flushes, and dizziness (Lewin & Gilmore,

Family Changes

In middle age, both sexes must make a shift in their way of living. When the last child leaves home, the parents sometimes feel lost and at loose ends. This has been called by some, the "empty next syndrome." It is more difficult for the woman because she spends more time in the home. It is especially hard if the children move far away, or if the woman is a widow or divorcee who has developed a strong emotional attachment to her children.

For middle-aged parents there must be a graceful retirement from child rearing. Other activities must be found to replace the child-centered duties that have occupied so many years. Some couples draw closer together, engage in more social activities, work at improving their homes, or become more active in church and community activities. Women often return to work or become active in clubs and other organizations.

But the readjustment to new middle-age roles is not always easy. It is difficult for women—even those who are trained for some vocation—to re-enter the labor force. Husbands and wives discover that they have grown apart during the child rearing years. The husband has become more involved in his work, the wife has become interested in family matters, and when they turn to each other for companionship after the children leave, some find that they have little in common. The pressures of the menopause, middle-age flings or infatuations, the loss of physical attractiveness, boredom with one's spouse, and the departure of children who have kept the marriage together, all contribute to increased marital difficulties during middle age. One study found that divorces are most likely to occur during the early twenties or during the forties (Glick & Landau, 1950).

When a couple has a good marriage, however there is a much easier adjustment to the problems of middle age. The husband and wife can find new warmth in their relationship, and work together in rounding out the years that are ahead. There is less need to worry about one's physical complaints or to interfere with the lives of one's children.

For the middle-aged person who is unmarried, family problems may be less demanding. Even so, the unmarried son or daughter often is given the added burden of caring for aged parents. This is frequently a thankless job which turns into loneliness when the parents die. Satisfactions· from one's work or outside activities sometimes lessen in middle age, and it may be difficult for the person to move into new social situations or to find satisfaction at home. However, in all of these adjustments, broad individual differences exist.

Vocational Problems

In the mid-forties, most adults are about half way through their working careers. For many, this is a time of great satisfaction. The individual is established in his work, producing at peak efficiency, and advancing to positions of greater responsibility and prestige. For others, however, middle age is a time of great frustration because they realize that they have not achieved what they had hoped—and that there is little likelihood of reaching life goals. Some react with bitterness and great disappointment. Others shift their aspirations to their children in hopes that "they will succeed where I didn't." Many, thinking of another twenty years in the labor force, experience vocational unrest and think about changing jobs—but this is not easy. It is difficult to find employment in middle age and a job change often means a reduction in salary accompanied by a loss in pension and other benefits. Most recognize that "there is nothing else to do," so they lower their aspirations, and settle in to the job they have. Even this may be a challenge. In our rapidly changing world, new skills and new knowledge are often needed so a person must be adaptable if he wants to hold his own (Super, 1957).

Even the people who succeed in their careers may experience frustration in middle life. Some conclude that they have chosen the wrong goals. Others who have been working toward some attainment or promotion, reach the desired end and experience a "promotion depression."

> Commonly. . .the man resents being burdened with a new load of responsibilities. He had striven to reach the goal, but the goal turns out to be something of an illusion. It is no haven but requires more work, more decision making, more responsibility. He cannot turn from it without loss of self esteem, but he resents the expectations others have for him, the demands of the boss or the organization, or his wife's ambitions that carried him beyond his limits (Litz, 1968, p. 462).

134

How do people react when they are dissatisfied with their work? Some escape into daydreams or alcohol, but most try to find satisfaction in activities outside of the job. Television, spectator sports, hobbies, and other pursuits provide the status and satisfaction that is not available elsewhere. But some find spare time too plentiful and boring. These people end up "killing time" in whatever way they can.

Religion and the Church in Middle Age

In general, very little is known about religion in middle age. Apparently, this age is a time of increased interest in religion, less concern about theological questions and renewed activity in the church. For many, the church is a source of comfort, happiness, satisfying fellowship, and opportunity for service.

In ministering to this group—as with all age groups—the church must be alert to individual needs. Even so there are some broad programs that would be welcomed by most middle-aged members of the congregation.

Vocational and Avocational Guidance

Since many persons are dissatisfied with their work, the church should provide opportunities for more satisfying service and activities. Included in this should be social events and opportunities for intellectual stimulation. In addition, the church leader can counsel with individual members concerning their jobs. If an individual can be helped to attain satisfaction in his vocational and avocational activities, he is much more likely to adjust happily to the middle years.

Marital and Family Guidance

A happy home life and a good marriage also contribute to satisfaction in the middle years. Seminars on marriage and family relations, sermons on the Christian home, and individual counseling can all be utilized by the church leader to bring about more satisfactory relationships in the home.

135

Helping People to Accept Adulthood

Since it is difficult for many to accept middle-age status, the church should help its members to find meaning and purpose in these years. The pastor can help his people to accept new roles, new responsibilities, and the realization that one is growing older.

Preparing for Old Age

Church leaders spend considerable time, effort and money preparing young children for the problems and responsibilities of adult life. Rarely, however, do we prepare people for the challenges of old age. The changes in physical condition, family status, and the work situation that begin in middle age, often extend into the later years. Christian education, therefore, need not stop when young people go off to college. The following conclusions by Kuhlen were not made with the church in mind, but they could be a stimulus for the development of creative educational programs in local congregations.

> Programs designed to foster continuous learning and broad participation in life *throughout the adult years* (in the 30's, 40's and 50's) will promote the development of the kinds of habits and personal resources (knowledge, skills, attitudes, and appreciations) which will make for good adjustment both at the present age and later in old age. . . . The most effective educational program. . .is broad and varied in scope and sensitive to the needs of all ages including those in the older years (Kuhlen, 1955, Quoted in Hurlock, 1959, p. 533).

A good way to begin this ministry is to form a committee of middle-aged persons who can decide on subject matter, design an effective program, and guide the pastor in his work with this age group.

For centuries, men have been concerned about old age. Early in Bible history Abraham was promised long life and "a good old age" (Genesis 15:15), apparently as something desirable. Wise King Solomon thought of old age as a time of glory, especially for righteous people (Proverbs 16:31). It was also recognized, however, that the end of life could be pleasant (Ecclesiastes 12:1). The Psalmist prayed that he would not be "cast off" or forsaken when he was old and weak (Psalm 71:9, 18). Many years later, Shakespeare gave a rather gloomy picture of the end of life.

> Last scene of all,
> That ends this strange eventful history
> Is second childishness, and mere oblivion
> Sans (without) teeth, sans eyes, sans taste,
>   sans everything.

It is not possible to discuss the "typical characteristics of old age." As with every other period in the life span, there are large individual differences in the ways people adjust to the later years. Compulsory retirement and pension programs would imply that old age begins when one turns sixty-five, but such a definition is arbitrary. Some people feel and act old when they are in their fifties, while others reach eighty and are "going strong" with few signs of slowing down. The individual's physical health, heredity, socioeconomic background, education, marital status, manner of living, mental alertness, attitude, and personality can all contribute to the speed with which he "ages."

Scientific interest in the study of aging is relatively new, having begun in earnest after the second world war. This upsurge of interest has probably arisen, in part, because of the increased life expectancy and the greater number of older people in our society. In the United States alone, people over sixty-five comprise ten per cent of the population, compared with two and a half per cent a century ago (*Time*, 1970). This increase in the number of people over sixty-five has important implications for church leaders. Since older people are becoming more and more prevalent in our churches, we must develop a greater understanding of the later years and find ways to minister more effectively to those who are senior citizens.

To appreciate the nature of old age, let us first consider three broad issues to which the older person must adapt more or less continuously: his slowly deteriorating physical condition, his changing roles and social status, and his plans for the future.

Physical Changes

The changes in body *appearance* that come with age are well known. There is a decrease in height and a stooping of the shoulders. Stiffness in the joints and disfigurations of the feet lead to difficulties in locomotion. The skin becomes dry, coarse and sagging, veins show clearly on the hands and legs; periodic tremors appear in the limbs and lower jaw; and the voice raises in pitch as speech becomes slower.

Less obvious are a number of changes within the body which influence the individual's *perceptual-motor functioning.* In order to interact with his environment a person must be able to (1) receive information through his sense organs; (2) organize and deal with this information by using his brain and other parts of the nervous system; and (3) react to the information by making movements of the bones and muscles. With advancing age, the function of all three levels declines. At stage one, *the perceptual,* there is a decline in the capacities of the sense organs. It becomes harder to see clearly—especially at low levels of illumination; the adaptation to changes in brightness is slower; sensitivity to color declines; the ability to hear high pitched sound decreases; sensitivity to touch and smell is reduced; and the taste buds become less sensitive (Weiss, 1959; Braum, 1959). At stage two, *the central nervous system,* reduced efficiency is evidenced by slower thinking, poorer memory —especially memory for recent events—and less efficient learning (Birren, 1964, 1970). This decline in the intellect begins in the 30's but that it is relatively insignificant until the 60's and 70's (Litz, 1968). At stage three, *the motor stage,* the older person finds that he cannot move as quickly as he once could. He finds a slowing in reaction time and a reduction in the accuracy of movements (Welford, 1959). This slowing down may also be reflected in a slowing of speech.

These changes in perceptual-motor functioning have some practical implications. After age sixty-five there is an increase in the number of falls and a sharp rise in the number of automobile accidents per 100,000 miles driven. In industry, it has been found that older people have far fewer accidents than younger people, but this is apparently because older workers are much more careful in their work. When they do have accidents, these are most often the result of falls or being hit by moving objects (Birren, 1964). Because of a slower reaction time, the older worker cannot "keep his balance or get out of the way" as quickly as the younger person.

With advancing age, there is also a decline in *health.* According to one writer, "health is a central factor in every aspect of the older person's life. It cuts across every social, occupational, and economic line. It affects every proposal for "improving the lot of older people" (Burney, 1956, vol. 71, p. 1168). In the later years, as other times in life, good health contributes to good adjustment and poor health interferes with adjustment. As one grows older, however, the amount and severity of illness increases. When the older person gets sick, his illness lasts for a longer period of time (Confrey and Goldstein, 1960). Broken bones are much slower to mend and injured tissue takes longer to heal.

Although the aged experience more physical difficulties and chronic illnesses than the young, the data indicate that the health of most older adults is reasonably good (Confrey and Goldstein, 1960). Their good health is partly because of advances in modern medicine, but the attitude of older people is important. While many show a tendency to complain about their ailments, others take their physical difficulties in stride. Since most tasks in life do not make maximum demands on our capacities, some deterioration is not particularly harmful. The pace may be a little slower but with extra effort and more attention being paid to details, the efficient performance of a task may be maintained, and sometimes even improved, in the presence of physical limitations (Birren, 1964).

Changing Status and Roles

Most people in our society look on old age with disfavor. Young adults are often critical of older people and don't want to have them around. One psychiatrist has even suggested that "age-ism" (a prejudice against "ugly old people") may in a few years become a problem equal to racism (*Time*, 1970). Even the aged themselves often regard the later years as a difficult and unrewarding time of life (Kastenbaum and Durke, 1964a, 1964b). This attitude leads to a reluctance to face the status of being a "senior citizen," but sometimes abrupt changes such as compulsory retirement or the loss of a spouse, force one to accept a new way of living. Other issues, such as the arrival of grandchildren, the death of friends, increasing loneliness, financial difficulties, or the problems of finding a place to live, slowly lead to the recognition that one is moving into a new status in life.

Let us begin with a look at *employment and retirement* in old age. If their health is good, older people want to continue working. In our society steady employment brings status, self respect, association with friends, a feeling of usefulness, and financial income. People in professions and skilled occupations are often very productive in their later years. Goethe, Verdi, Titian, and more recently Picasso, Grandma Moses, Eisenhower, and Churchill are examples. Those who work in salaried jobs after age sixty-five are less likely to be absent from work, and remain on a job longer than younger workers. Furthermore they apparently show no noticeable decline in productivity (McFarland and O'Doherty, 1959).

Unfortunately, however, it is almost impossible for people to find work after age sixty-five. Our society is changing so rapidly that skills become outdated and employers prefer to train younger men to fill new jobs. Because of higher insurance and other costs, it is expensive to retain older workers. In an effort to treat everyone alike, many employees have a policy of compulsory retirement at age sixty-five.

In adjusting to retirement, most people go through three stages. First, is the "project" period. People take a long desired trip, fix-up the house, move to another location, or work on some project that they have been putting off for a long time. Second, comes a period of restlessness. After completing the projects, the retired person starts looking for something to do. He tries to find new purpose in life and new goals. He must learn to see himself in the role of a "retired person" or "pensioner." Most people clear this obstacle within a year after retirement and settle down to stage three—the period of stable adjustment to retirement. During this time the retired person carries out the roles of his new status (Havighurst, 1955). He establishes a new pattern for spending the day, makes new friends, engages in new activities, and learns to live with a smaller budget.

There are individual differences in the ease with which one adjusts to retirement. In general, adjustment is smoother when the retired person is healthy, has socially meaningful activities, had a positive pre-retirement attitude toward retirement, had made preparation for retirement before it occured, is not overly dependent, and is relatively secure economically (Donahue, et. al., 1960).

The later years often bring great *economic difficulties* since retirement income is usually less than what was earned on the job. As medical expenses get higher and the cost of living rises steadily, the older person has greater and greater difficulty making ends meet, especially if he is on a fixed-income pension. It usually is not feasible to think about part-time work so there must be a cutting back in expenses. This often leads to a poorer diet or less desirable housing.

This issue of *housing* is yet another problem area for many older people. In the past, many people remained in the same house for most of their lives. If health began to fail, a daughter often moved in to the "old homestead" to help until the parent died. Today things are much different! A couple may spend many years buying a home but when the children leave it is found that the home is too large and costly to maintain. If one of the parents dies, and/or there is a decline in health, it becomes necessary to sell the home. But where is the older person to live? In our mobile society, grown-up children are often far away. They have growing families, and because of the high cost of real estate, may have limited space. Even when extra room is available, families are reluctant to establish a three-generation household since this often leads to conflict. Nursing homes for the elderly are sometimes available but the costs are high and the services are often poor. Little wonder that many people resist such moves, especially if the nursing homes are far away from a familiar neighborhood and long-time friends. The personality characteristics, health, economic status, and social class of the older person and his family will all affect the way in which the housing problem is solved.

Probably one of the biggest and most abrupt adjustments of any age comes with the *loss of a spouse.* Even when death was expected, widowhood involves a new status, loneliness, and an abrupt change in one's manner of living.

In our society, women prefer to marry men who are the same age or a little older. Since men usually die at an earlier age than women, it is most often the wife who must face the emotional strain and adjustment problems of living without a spouse. Following the death of a loved one, among the first issues that must be faced are selection of a casket and arrangements for the funeral. Later, the widow must go through her husband's possessions. She must learn to live with overwhelming loneliness; take responsibility for hospital bills, funeral expenses, and mortgage payments; make decisions about housing, children (sometimes), and the problems of living on a reduced budget; and she must learn to live alone in a society that is centered around couples. One widow described this problem as follows:

> Like the animals on Noah's ark, adults travel in pairs. Old friends, understandably concerned with their own families, their own jobs, their own social life, simply evaporate. The. . .widow is cruelly cut out of the herd by most of her friends and neighbors at the very time when she needs them most. . . .I must face the fact that I am outside normal society (Murray and Cort, 1961, p. 146).

Since we do not like to face the implications of death any sooner than we have to, prior preparations for widowhood are rare. In the midst of grief the surviving spouse must often make important decisions which could have been discussed while the husband and wife were still together. Clearly, preparation for widowhood, and help in adjusting to life alone, are major responsibilities of the church (James 1:27).

Aging has been described as an "inevitable mutual withdrawal or *disengagement"* in which the older person slowly withdraws from society, and the society withdraws from the individual. This mutual withdrawal is a slow process that varies from person to person. By disentangling himself from life, the older person prepares himself for the future so that he eventually will be able to "slip from life almost unnoticed" (Cumming and Henry, 1961). This brings us to the third major issue which must be dealt with in later life.

Facing the Future

The older person must recognize that life is coming to an end. He has raised his children and made his contribution to society. Now he must prepare for the future. This involves a review of life's accomplishments and failures, a consideration of the meaning of life and goals for the remaining years; and a facing of the approach of death.

The *life review* in old age has been described as a "naturally-occurring universal mental process" (Butler, 1964, p. 266). At times, all of us look back on our lives, and contemplate our experiences, accomplishments and failures. This is especially likely when we are facing problems, decisions, or crises. For the older person, retirement, loss of a spouse, the departure of the last child, failing health, or the realization that the end of life is approaching can all stimulate a reflection on the life that one has lived. A few older persons review their lives in an orderly, logical manner and write autobiographies, but for most people the life review is a very casual experience. Often the older person is only vaguely aware that it is even taking place.

Frequently, the life review leads to nostalgia for "the good old days," a lot of talk about the past, and feelings of regret over former actions or failures. For many, the life review brings increased candor, serenity, and wisdom. For some, it brings depression, guilt, anxiety and despair. This is especially true for people who have been arrogant, self-centered, proud and inconsiderate (Butler, 1964). Such people apparently are dissatisfied with their lives and see

144

no way of reversing their behavior in the years that remain. Although the life review is a normal experience, it influences people in different ways.

The *meaning and purpose of life* in the later years also differs from person to person. For some, perhaps a third of all older people (Cavan, et. al., 1949), these may be "golden years" or "fulfillment years" (Stamats, 1968), but for most this is a time of loneliness and despair. Our modern western society does not do much to make the older person feel useful or wanted — and because things are changing so quickly, his wisdom, opinion, and experience is neither sought nor desired. What, then, is the purpose for living in old age?

A few years ago, a study was reported which had investigated the goals of aging people in a variety of different cultures (Simmons, 1946). It was concluded that most older persons want:

• *To live as long as possible* — or at least until life is no longer satisfying and the advantages of death seem to outweigh the burden of life (Kuhlen, 1959).

• *To maintain one's health* — which involves getting sufficient rest and exercise, avoiding physical hazards, and preserving one's energies.

• *To remain active* — people do not want to be idle. They would rather be busy, preferably in activities which are socially useful and mentally stimulating. The older person, therefore, must find satisfying leisure activities (Kaplan, 1959).

• *To keep and strengthen the skills, possessions, rights, authorities, prestige, and other prerogatives that have been acquired during life.* Older people, for example, are unhappy if they are rejected or ignored by their families. They are eager to maintain contact and participate in family affairs. Unfortunately, however, some oldsters encourage family dissention because they want to dominate and control their grown-up children.

• *To withdraw from life, when necessary, as honorably as possible.* This includes a minimum of suffering at the end, and hope for an attractive afterlife.

In facing death, the individual is confronted with several major tasks (Aldrich 1966, Birren, 1964). First, he must accept his physical symptoms and the permanent limitations that they impose. Secondly, he must adjust to the realization that he will soon be separated from loved ones and friends. This realization often brings sadness in anticipation of the loss. Thirdly, if he has not already done so, he must review his life and in some cases accept the fact that what he wanted to achieve may never come. Fourthly, he must get his economic affairs in order. This task may be easier for the older person who has mainly disengaged himself from society, than for the younger person who has many family and financial concerns. Sometimes, however, people are reluctant to draw up a will because it is too painful to face this tangible evidence of coming death. Finally, the dying person must face the prospect of life after death. For some, this brings uncertainty and fear. For the believer in Jesus Christ death is something to be desired. It brings a certainty of being "with Christ" and this is "far better" than life on earth (Philippians 1:21-24).

Older People and the Church

Do older people turn to religion as a source of comfort in the later years? This is a widely held belief but the available research indicates that in general, interest in religion does *not* increase with age. Instead, old people carry on the beliefs and practices that they held earlier in life. Those who have been religious all their lives, are religious in old age; those who have not been religious in the earlier years show no tendency to become more religious in later life (Maves, 1960).

When questioned about their attitudes toward the church, older people express a number of dissatisfactions. Many feel that they are neglected by the church, or pushed aside by younger members. The widespread belief is that church programs are planned for young people and that the older members are "excess baggage" who really don't fit. Some feel that they cannot afford to dress well enough or contribute enough to be accepted by church congregations. Others find that poor health, difficulties in getting transportation to and from the church, or problems with the physical features of the church building (such as long staircases, poor accoustics, or "hard-to-get-to" washrooms) lead them to withdraw from active participation in church activities (Gray and Moberg, 1962).

In spite of the obstacles involved, the church has a responsibility for ministering to the needs of the elderly. In the Bible, especially the Old Testament, long life and old age is recognized as something desirable. It is considered as a gift from God, especially for those who are His obedient servants (I Kings 3:14; Psalms 91:16; Proverbs 10:27). Younger people are instructed to respect and care for those who are older (Leviticus 19:32; Proverbs 23:22; I Timothy 5:1,2) and God Himself promises to be present with the elderly among His people (Isaiah 46:4). There are even some biblical guidelines concerning how older people ought to act (I Peter 3:10, Titus 2:2,3).

Recently, a number of reports have considered ways in which church leaders and their congregations can minister to the elderly (Brown, 1968; Culver, 1961; Gray and Moberg, 1962; Maves and Cedarleaf, 1949; Special Staff on Aging, 1961). Specific suggestions include the following:

The church can help people to adjust to old age. As indicated earlier in the chapter, this should begin in middle age. By helping younger people anticipate the problems and challenges of the later years, the adjustments to aging can be made much easier. When the individual does reach the age of retirement, when he (or she) loses a spouse, when loneliness, sickness or economic hardships arise, the church can provide counsel, encouragement, emotional support, and practical assistance. Individual counseling, group discussions, and sermons or lectures can all be used to facilitate this adjustment to aging.

The church can minister to the spiritual needs of older people. As a person reviews his life, and as he considers the future, including death, he can look for the church to provide encouragement and re-assurance. For some, of course, old age is the period of life when Christ is first accepted as Savior and Lord. Because of this, the church must be concerned about evangelism among the aged. For all believers, the later years provide opportunity for spiritual growth and for contemplation of the "mansions" that Christ has prepared for those who believe in Him (John 14:1-6). Even in old age, the Christian can experience an earthly life that is abundant and serene (John 10:10; 14:27; Isaiah 26:3). This spiritual strength is especially important when physical health is failing or when the older person meets the crises and problems that accompany the later years.

The church can provide companionship and opportunities for useful service. Even as they disengage from society, older people need to have some social outlets and a place where they really feel welcome. Some churches not only attempt to keep older people involved in the life of the parish, but also provide special tours and activities that broaden the older person's social contacts and usefulness (Stamats, 1968). The goal in programs for older people can not be simply to fill time; the participants in such programs want to be doing things that are socially useful. Table 5-1 summarizes some of the practical ways in which older people can contribute to the church.

When possible, older people should be integrated into existing church groups. This is because people are sometimes reluctant to enroll in new groups that are identified

148

Table 5—1

What Older People Can Do For The Church*

1. Participate in worship services as a participant and/or as a leader.
2. Teach others.
3. Assist in the visitation program.
4. Help to improve and maintain church property.
5. Assist with minor but vital service tasks, e.g. preparation of food for social gatherings, directing traffic in the parking lot, writing to missionaries and other absent members, sewing, etc.
6. Help with the clerical work.
7. Serve as advisor in various church groups.
8. Be a counselor who listens, supports, encourages, and guides.
9. Support the church program in prayer.
10. Engage in their own personal devotional activities.

*Adapted from R. M. Gray and D. O. Moberg, *The Church and the Older Person,* Eerdmans, 1962; and Special Staff on Aging, *Religion and Aging,* U. S. Government Printing Office, 1961.

as organizations for old people. An existing Sunday school class or sewing circle can sometimes be expanded into a broader program. If separate programs for older people do exist, these should be person-centered rather than activity-centered; should be run by the older persons themselves; should be characterized by shared responsibilities; and should deal with the interests of the group members. Such interests can often be determined by checklists or questionnaires. The group members can also keep in touch with former participants and other older persons who are not able to participate (Gray and Moberg, 1962).

The church can educate. Special lectures, discussion groups, Bible studies, films and other educational programs can provide intellectual stimulation for the older mind. It is not just the older church member who needs education about aging. In their excellent little book Gray and Moberg (1962) suggest that the church leader can educate his entire congregation by dispelling some common misconceptions about aging and old people. These misconceptions include the idea that:

- old people are nearly all the same;
- old people are rigid and no longer able to grow, to learn, or adjust to new circumstances;
- old age is a useless period when the individual can no longer be active and is unable to make any useful contribution to the church or to society;
- old people have no interest in sex;
- old people want to run everything and to prevent younger people from having any responsibility.

While each of these is true of *some* older people, such statements do not apply to the majority. Undoubtedly, the attitudes, opinions, and problems of aging can best be shared if older persons themselves are involved in the educational program. When younger members respect and attempt to understand older people, the congregation has taken a major step toward ministering to its senior members.

The church can meet the physical needs of older persons. Christians have a God-given responsibility to care for persons with practical needs (James 1:27). Providing food, helping with shopping, mowing lawns or shoveling snow, providing transportation to and from church—are all ways in which older people can be helped. Such projects are especially beneficial to young people's groups within the church.

The church should also have adequate facilities for aged members. Good heating, non-glare lighting, skid-proof floor wax, an adequate public address system, "easy to read" print in hymnbooks or other literature, and pews from which it is easy to rise, are all important. In addition, rest rooms should be in locations that are easily reached, and long flights of stairs should be avoided. Wherever there are stairs, there should be sturdy railings. At first glance it may appear that to provide all of these facilities would require construction of a new ediface. On the contrary, many of these can be provided in existing buildings with a minimum of expense.

Summary

In a society which emphasizes the desirability of youth, adjustments to the latter half of life are often very difficult. In middle age, people must accept the fact that there are changes in physical appearance, abilities, and health. There must be an adjustment to the "empty nest" from which the children have gone, and a new appraisal of one's goals and purposes in life. With retirement comes the realization that a useful place in society has been lost. The aging individual must accept "senior citizen" status with the loneliness, financial stress, and physical decline that it so often brings.

The modern church has stressed the Christian education of youth, but middle and old age largely has been neglected. As greater numbers of people survive into the later years, church leaders must develop a greater concern and understanding of the needs and capabilities of the people who are over forty. Church facilities and programs must be designed with the older person in mind. The present chapter has given some practical suggestions concerning how this might be done.

Chapter Six

MAKING THE BEST OF STRESS

January of 1967, like most northern winters, was a cold month in St Paul, Minnesota. Record snow falls had deposited almost eight feet of snow on the area, and sub-zero temperatures had prevented most of this from melting. On a morning in early February the people who lived near the Minnesota State Fairgrounds felt a great rumble which shook the foundations of their houses. One of the largest and newest buildings in the fairgrounds had buckled under the weight of the snow and collapsed into a mass of twisted steel, cement, wood, ice and snow. Nobody was injured in the collapse—the building was empty—and the event attracted only local interest. Within a few hours, however, State Fair officials and insurance adjustors began an investigation, which subsequently revealed that the building had collapsed because of poor construction, and the *stress* of ice and snow.

Originally, stress was a term used only by engineers and architects. The word referred to a force which put such pressure on an object that the object was altered in some way. In Minnesota, the building (object) was destroyed (which is certainly an alteration) by the stress (force) of the ice and snow. Later the term stress came to be used in a much broader sense. Physical stress, emotional stress, social stress, psychological stress, and similar phrases were used to describe forces that put pressure on living organisms.

As used in this chapter, stress refers to an influence or stimulus which exerts force on a person. The stress may come from the external environment or from inside the individual. It may be mild, of moderate intensity, or so severe that it poses a strong danger to the well being of the person. At times it can lead to a physical or psychological collapse.

If we never encountered stress, life would be simple — and also pretty dull. For most people, however, stress is a common experience. Every day we meet influences which in some way alter our behavior. In this chapter we will consider the sources of this stress, discuss some ways in which stress is handled, and show how this relates to the work of the church.

The Sources Of Stress

A situation is stressful if it hinders, makes difficult, or causes failure in some activity. Such every day experiences as noise, distractions, competition, a lack of time, or a difficult problem can all be stressful (Korchin, 1963). For purposes of classification, however, psychologists usually divide stresses into three categories: those which arise from frustrations, those resulting from conflicts, and those which stem from pressures.

Frustrations

Frustration results when our progress toward some desirable goal is blocked (see Fig. 6-1). The term "frustration" can refer either to the obstacle that impedes progress, or to the feeling that occurs when an obstacle is encountered. It is possible, therefore, to talk about frustrating situations, and frustrated people.

Frustrations are of two types, external and internal. *External frustrations* are obstacles in the environment. All of us have experienced rain at a picnic, a pen that runs dry

154

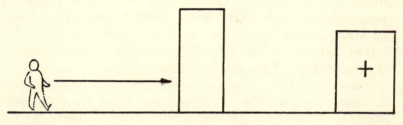

individual   obstacle   goal

Figure 6—1

Frustration. The individual's progress
toward some desired (positive) goal is
blocked by an interferring obstacle.

in the middle of a signature, or a flat tire when we are in a
hurry. Of greater intensity are the frustrations which result
when a draft board refuses to grant a deferment, a girl says
"no" to a marriage proposal, a bank turns down a loan application, a Sunday school class is uncontrollable, or the
members of the congregation ignore the pastor's invitation
to go calling on people in the neighborhood. *Internal
frustrations* refer to personal limitations within the individual.
These could include physical handicaps, a low opinion of
one's self, social incompetence, or a lack of desired training. The student of below average ability who wants to be a
physician, the "wrong" color skin for a person who wants to
live in some segregated area, or small-body build in a boy
who wants to play football, are all examples of frustrations
resulting from internal limitations.

155

Conflicts

Almost every adult has had the experience of being forced to decide between two or more mutually exclusive, but equally desirable goals. This is a conflict. A woman who likes two hats, but can only afford to buy one is in such a situation. As with frustration, "conflict" can refer to the external circumstances (such as the two hats), or to the internal feelings that an individual experiences as he weighs the alternatives. Conflicts are of three types.

Approach-approach conflict arises when the incompatable goals are equally attractive and the individual is torn between the desirable alternatives (see Fig. 6-2). The woman in the hat shop is in this kind of a conflict, and so is the student who wants to take anthropology and sociology but discovers that they both meet at the same hour. Most people resolve this kind of conflict by choosing one goal and trying to forget the other.

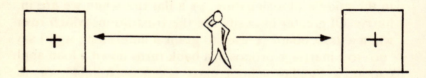

Figure 6—2

Approach-approach conflict. The individual feels drawn to two desirable but mutually exclusive alternatives.

Avoidance-avoidance conflict results when one is faced with two equally undesirable alternatives (see Fig. 6-3). When a mother tells her young daughter to "eat your spinach or go without desert" the child is in an avoidance-avoidance conflict. The child either eats spinach or misses desert—both alternatives are undesirable but she must choose one. Similarly, the person with a toothache who does not like pain but also dislikes dentists, is in this kind of a conflict. In these situations there is often considerable vascillation and creative attempts to avoid selecting one of the alternatives.

Figure 6—3

Avoidance-avoidance conflict. The individual feels repelled by undesirable alternatives.

Approach-avoidance conflict occurs when a goal has both desirable and undesirable features at the same time (see Fig. 6-4). The pastor who is called to a large church may want to serve in this greater area of influence, but may at the same time want to turn down the invitation because he feels insecure and in doubt about his ability to handle

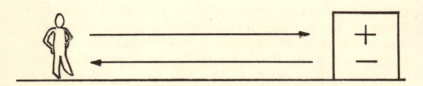

Figure 6—4

Approach-Avoidance Conflict. The individual feels drawn to and repelled from a
situation which has both desirable and
undesirable features.

the job. Many people experience approach-avoidance
conflict as they contemplate marriage. There is a desire
for a warm and loving relationship with a spouse, but a
fear that marriage might interfere with one's freedom,
career aspirations or travel plans.

This is perhaps the most common type of conflict. It leads
to great vascillation and indecision. The attractive features
of the situation draw us to it, but the unattractive ones
bounce us back (Arkoff, 1968).

In every day living, few conflicts fit concisely into one
of these three categories. The decisions of life are usually
more complex. The pastor who is called to the large church,
for example, may really be facing multiple conflicts
(see Fig. 6-5). There may be both desirable and undesirable
features connected with (a) staying in his present position
(b) moving to a larger church or, perhaps (c) leaving the
pastorate altogether and teaching in a seminary.

158

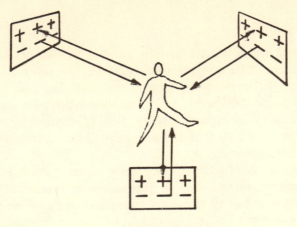

Figure 6—5

Multiple approach-avoidance conflicts. The individual faces a number of courses of action, each of which has several desirable (attracting) and undesirable (repelling) features (Adapted from A.Arkoff, *Adjustment and Mental Health.* McGraw-Hill, 1968).

Pressures

Sometimes people experience demands that push them toward a certain type of behavior. These demands, which are usually termed "pressures," may arise from external or internal sources.

External pressures come from other people or from the situation in which we are living. Parents pressure their children to get higher grades, teachers give assignments and deadlines which put pressure on their students, and religious leaders sometimes pressure their congregation to "make decisions for Christ." Probably everyone has heard of the "high pressure salesman" who tries to push prospective customers into making a purchase. Sometimes the pressure comes from a number of less specific sources. The young mother who struggles to maintain a home and keep the kids happy, or the business executive who must make many important decisions, or examples of persons who feel pressure from the environment.

Internal pressures are usually related to our ambitions or self-image. The student who feels he must get all A's, the soldier who wants to be a hero, the musician who wants to have a perfect concert, or the author who feels pushed to write a novel of highest quality, are influenced by internal pressures—all of which have been learned during the course of one's lifetime.

Frustration, conflict, and pressure often combine in a given stress situation. Let us return to the preacher who is deciding whether to move to a larger church. Since any decision has both favorable and unfavorable features, the pastor is in a multiple conflict situation. Assume, however, that in addition the other congregation is anxious for an immediate decision, and that the present congregation is urging him not to "leave such a thriving work." To these pressures might be added the frustration of wanting God's leading, but not yet knowing it. With important decisions, the stress may be great because all three sources are often present.

Severity Of Stress

All stress is not severe; some is relatively minor. According to one psychologist (Coleman, 1964), the severity of a stressful situation can be determined by considering several questions.

How long has the stress persisted? When stress lasts for a long period it tends to become more and more severe. For one night we can tolerate a loud radio playing until midnight in the next apartment. If the radio is on every night until three a.m., however, the stress (and anger) becomes more intense. Research studies have shown that even a mild stress which persists for a long time is more of a strain than an intense but brief stress (Torrance, 1965).

How important is the stress? Conflict over whether or not to marry is likely to be more important and hence more stressful than conflict over whether or not to have a second cup of coffee after dinner.

How many stresses are operating at a given time? Stresses which might be easy to handle one at a time, may be very difficult to handle if they all occur at once. If the dinner guests arrive, the telephone rings, the baby cries, and the timer sounds on the oven—all at the same time—the hostess is likely to feel great stress (to put it mildly) especially if her husband has not yet arrived home from work.

Are the conflicting forces of nearly equal strength? If so, the conflict is likely to be more intense and difficult to resolve.

How does the individual look at the situation? People perceive situations differently and react in accordance with their perceptions. Two girls in love may view a broken engagement in different ways. For one it may be a source of intense frustration accompanied by feelings of failure, inadequacy, and humiliation. Another may feel hurt, but also be grateful that the incompatibility became known before the marriage rather than afterwards. Obviously, the broken engagement is more stressful for the first girl.

How much stress resistance does the individual have? "Stress tolerance" or "frustration tolerance" refers to the intensity of stress that a person can experience without undergoing a breakdown in his behavior. Apparently, there are considerable individual differences in this ability to withstand stress. What is greatly stressful for one person may be less stressful for another. Some writers have even suggested that mental health involves not only functioning adequately in general but also having the ability to get along effectively while under stress (Korchin, 1963).

Reactions to Stress

The severity of stress determines, in large measure, how one will react. As shown in figure 6-6, mild stress leads to improved psychological functioning, better learning, and greater effeciency. It is not until stress becomes intense, however, that there is a deterioration in one's behavior (Torrance, 1965). To put this in more practical terms, students (including those in the Sunday school) learn best if there is some pressure, but not too much. Overly permissive child rearing, and overly harsh techniques, can both be harmful for a child, but a mild amount of stress is healthy.

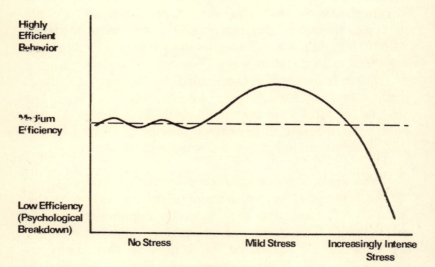

Figure 6—6

Efficiency of performance under stress of differing intensity (Adapted from E. P. Torrance, *Constructive Behavior: Stress, Personality and Mental Health,* Wadsworth, 1965).

162

It is possible to identify two broad types of stress. The first is the brief, but intense stress that comes in emergency situations; the second is a moderate but more long-lasting stress. Our reactions to these two kinds of stresses tend to be different. In the first case, we mobilize all of our energies, to deal with the threatening situation, but when the crisis passes, we return to a more normal state. Short-term stress taxes our energies, but with time we are usually able to recover. In contrast, long term stress is usually more demanding. Instead of mobilizing our resources for a short burst of energy, we must resist for a long period. With little chance to rest and recover our strength, long term resistance can be very exhausting.

Reactions to stress are both physical and psychological. While we will separate these for purposes of discussion, it should be remembered that the whole organism responds to stress: The physical and psychological reactions occur together, not in isolation.

Physical Reactions to Stress

Several years ago, a researcher named Hans Selye (1956, 1969) suggested that physical reactions to stress occur in three stages. First, is the stage of "alarm and mobilization." The heart beats faster, breathing becomes more rapid, digestive processes slow down, muscles become tense, and the individual becomes more alert.

These physical reactions enable the body to handle short-term stress following which there is a relatively rapid return to a more normal physiological state. When the stress persists a stage of "resistance" begins in which the body prepares to cope with prolonged stress and attempts at the same time to maintain some kind of physiological balance. If the stress continues, strength eventually may be depleted, the individual is no longer able to resist and the stage of "exhaustion" and collapse occurs. Recovery from the effects of such prolonged stress is often very slow (Torrance, 1965).

Psychological Reactions to Stress

The physiological stress reactions are accompanied by a number of psychological reactions. As little children, each of us learns how to cope with stress, but we don't all learn to cope in the same way (Murphy, 1962). Because of these different experiences in childhood, people differ in how they react to stress as adults, but even in spite of these variations, it is possible to identify some common psychological reactions. These are of two broad types: task-directed reactions and defensive reactions.

Task-directed Reactions: In many stressful situations, we try to tackle the problem directly and handle it in a realistic way. To do so, we must define the problem, work out possible solutions, decide on the most suitable course of action, try this out, and evaluate the results of our efforts. Sometimes two or more possible solutions are tried before we find one which is effective. In tackling a problem directly, we sometimes precede in a conscious, logical, step by step way, but things need not always be that clearcut. Even if we are vague in our thinking and hesitating in our responses, it is possible (although less probable) to directly handle a stress with competence.

The most common task-directed reactions are attack, withdrawal, and compromise. *Attack* involves an attempt to remove or surmount the stressful situation. The minister who feels pressure because he does not have a sermon prepared, can attack the problem by locking himself in the study and working on the message. The prisoner of war who is under the stress of confinement might plan a method for escape.

When one moves to overcome a stress, the possibility of failure is always present. Attacking a problem, therefore, always involves taking a risk (Torrance, 1965). Of course the risk is greater in some situations than in others. If the risk is small, attack may be a good way to handle a stress. If the risk is very great, attack might best be avoided.

164

The prisoner of war, for example may decide that he is likely to get caught if he tries to escape. In such a case, attack may be too risky and too costly a solution to the problem.

Withdrawal can be either physical or psychological. The person who is losing an argument, may leave the room (graciously if possible) or he may rely on such psychological techniques as changing the subject, admitting defeat, conveniently forgetting "what I was going to say," or suggesting that "we discuss this more later" in hopes that the subject will never come up again. By withdrawing from a stressful situation, the person is "unloading" or getting rid of a difficulty.

Sometimes total and permanent withdrawal is possible, but when this cannot be done, even a temporary drawing apart can be helpful. By taking a short vacation, laying an issue aside for a while, or discussing it with a friend, the individual often can return to face the stress with new vigor and efficiency.

In writing this book, the author periodically finds that he cannot form words and phrases to express what he wants to say. At such times, a short walk around the room or a skimming over what has been written previously, provides a temporary withdrawal which is then followed (sometimes) by a new burst of ideas. Occasionally I leave the manuscript altogether for a while and go for coffee or for a time of browsing through a magazine. At such times there is, of course, the danger of being distracted and not returning to my work. For the minister preparing a sermon, the student writing a term paper, or the author working on a book, withdrawal must be only temporary if the task is to be completed.

Compromise involves a reduction of stress that comes from the changing of ones aspirations, expectations or activities. A student who is getting poorer grades than he expected may lower his aspirations and settle for C's. A husband and wife may make concessions to each other in order to bring better family relations. Likewise, disagreeing groups will sometimes arrive at a "bargain" in which each gives in a little to the others' demands.

"Compromise" is often thought of as something bad. Sometimes compromise does involve weakness and the lowering of one's standards, but at other times, compromise is a wise and effective way of handling a stress.

Hope is another way of coping with the stresses of life. When he hopes, the individual takes "bits of reality" and ties them together by logic, reasoning and expectation (Korner, 1970; Frank, 1968). He has something to cling to, something that will keep him from despair and motivate him to press on in spite of the difficulties of the situation. Hope is an important characteristic for all men and especially for those who have hope because they are "in Christ" (Cleath, 1970).

Then there is *prayer* and a reliance on the leading and intervention of God. For the Christian this is a crucial and a very practical way of tackling a difficult situation. The Christian believes that God hears prayer and answers, sometimes through divine intervention in stressful situations. At other times, the Holy Spirit guides men as they deal with their problems (John 16:13). Most psychology textbooks do not mention the influence of the supernatural, but this is a significant force in the life of the believer.

Defensive Reactions: Several years ago, an emotionally disturbed student mounted a tower at a university in the south and began taking potshots at the people below. When the bullets began flying, the passersby quickly ran for cover. They squated behind cars, ran into buildings, or dashed wherever there was a protective defense against the danger.

In dealing with the stresses of life we are sometimes unable or unwilling to tackle the problem directly. At other times we may try to remove a stress, but fail. On these occasions, like the people on the southern campus, we take cover in order to defend ourselves. Instead of running behind buildings, we develop defensive ways of thinking which protect us from anxiety, soften failures, and preserve self-esteem. These ways of thinking, which psychologists call *defensive mechanisms,* are rarely used deliberately. More often, they are unconscious reactions.

Defensive reactions are used at times by almost everyone. They are not necessarily bad, although they can be unwise in some circumstances. In one situation, for example, defensive thinking may protect a person from the anxiety which might otherwise overwhelm him. At another time, the defensive reaction may prevent the individual from facing and solving a problem that he could handle well (Arkoff, 1968).

Although psychologists have suggested as many as thirty defensive mechanisms, only a few of the more common of these are listed below. The church leader in all probability will have seen many of these in himself and/or in his congregation.

Rationalization is the making of logically-sounding excuses in an attempt to justify something that we have done or failed to do. We may be going seventy-five in a sixty-mile-an-hour zone, but tell ourselves "its okay because everyone else is doing it." The over-weight lady may take a big dessert because "everyone should splurge once in a while." Sometimes Christians engage in sin and then rationalize their behavior by concluding "we must be 'one of the boys' if we are going to be a real witness for Christ."

Repression involves the exclusion from conscious awareness of all those desires, impulses, thoughts, and ideas that are threatening. The church organist who plays a sour note during the offertory, or the young preacher who gives a poor sermon may put the memory of these unpleasant and embarrassing experiences out of their minds.

167

Regression occurs when an adult reacts to stress in a way which was successfully used to avoid unpleasant situations at an earlier time in life. When a new baby enters a home, older children sometimes return to baby talk or bed wetting in an apparent attempt to get attention. Some adults find that sulking or crying gets them out of a stressful situation—just like it did when they were children.

Projection involves blaming someone else for the motives and weaknesses that are really our own. A student who fails a test because of his lack of ability or preparation, may push the blame on to the professor's "poor lectures" or the textbook's "lack of clarity." Intolerant church members usually deny their own lack of tolerance, but are quick to accuse members of other denominations of being rigid and intolerant.

Displacement often results as a response to frustration. Instead of directing our feelings toward the source of our frustrations, we channel feelings instead toward some less threatening person or object. The man who is bawled out by his boss may in turn "let off steam" by yelling at his secretary.

Fantasy is a retreat from stressful reality and a move into some kind of dream world. Relaxing with a novel, watching a movie on television, or daydreaming about some fanciful happenings, are widely used fantasy activities.

Reaction Formation is an attempt to hide or squelch one type of impulse by stressing the opposite. Suppose a member of the congregation is complaining, demanding and bothersome to the extent that the pastor feels resentment and annoyance. Since pastors are supposed to be kind and sympathetic, instead of telling the parishioner to "get lost —and stop bothering me"—(which is the way he feels), the pastor may do the exact opposite. He listens, sympathizes, and encourages the person to "call me at any time." Sometimes people who are strongly attracted to sex magazines become militant crusaders *against* "obscene literature on our newsstands." Those who would really like to be dirty and messy sometimes are excessively neat and clean instead. In each of these situations, the person defends himself against his real feelings by stressing the opposite.

It should not be assumed, of course, that sympathetic pastors, pornography opponents, or neat people are always showing the opposite of their real feelings. How then, do we distinguish reaction formations from nonreactive traits? The reaction formation is characterized by three unique qualities. First, the behavior is excessive, and sometimes used to a ridiculous extent. The person who is preoccupied with cleanliness and more concerned about it than anyone else, for example, may be showing a defensive reaction. Shakespeare expressed this in *Hamlet*. "Me thinks," he wrote, "the lady doth protest too much." This excessive protest was a hint about her real feelings. Secondly, in defensive reactions, the objectionable impulse occasionally breaks through the facade. The overly meticulous person may occasionally get very dirty. Thirdly, the person reacts with strong feelings if the reaction behavior is blocked. The meticulous person may be very annoyed or anxious, if the water is shut off or if for some other reason, he cannot be clean and neat (Rosen and Gregory, 1965).

Identification involves taking on the characteristics of some person whom we admire. The young seminary student who is not doing very well in his first attempts at preaching, may consciously or unconsciously imitate and take on the characteristics of some successful preacher whom he admires. Little children usually identify with their parents and sometimes parents identify with their successful children.

169

In each case we reduce the stress of facing our weaknesses by becoming like someone whom we see as being in a more desirable situation.

Malingering is the removal of stress by consciously or unconsciously feigning illness. When we are sick, we have a socially acceptable excuse for avoiding the stresses of life. If the stresses are especially intense, it may be handy to appear sick. This often has an added "fringe benefit." In addition to removal of unwanted stress, sickness can bring attention and sympathy.

Collapse—Sometimes, stress is so great that a person can neither deal with it, nor defend himself against it. In such situations, the individual "breaks down" and is no longer able to function efficiently. This collapse, which is sometimes called "mental illness" or "abnormal behavior," will be discussed in detail in a later book of this series entitled, *The Fractured Personality.*

Anxiety and Stress

The twentieth century has been called "the age of anxiety. ' In the opinion of some psychologists, anxiety is "the official emotion" of our time, the "most pervasive psychological phenomenon" of modern society and the emotion of "central significance" in all abnormal behavior (Levitt, 1967).

Anxiety is an emotional state that comes as a result of stress and is characterized by apprehension, uneasiness, and fear. Sometimes anxiety arises when we are aware of a recognizable threat. At other times we feel anxious, but cannot find any reason for our feelings. Some people are anxious almost all the time; others are relatively free from anxiety, except in very stressful situations. Anxiety may be so intense that a person is immobilized, or it may be so mild that it is hardly noticed. It can be conscious or unconscious. It can interfere with our activities, as in stagefright, or it can spur us on to greater efforts, as happens when anxiety about a test causes us to study harder. Apparently too little anxiety can be almost as harmful as too much.

The church leader is most likely to observe anxiety when he is visiting with the sick and their families. The prospect of surgery, the coming of death, and even the need to visit the dentist are stresses that can result in great anxiety. According to one psychologist who studied surgical patients,

> . . .a major. . .operation constitutes a stress situation which resembles many other types of catastrophes and disasters in that the 'victim' faces a combination of three major forms of imminent danger—the possibility of suffering acute pain, of undergoing serious body damage, and of dying (Janis, 1958, p. 10).

Anxiety in the patient increases as the surgery approaches and then drops during the recovery period (see Figure 6-7).

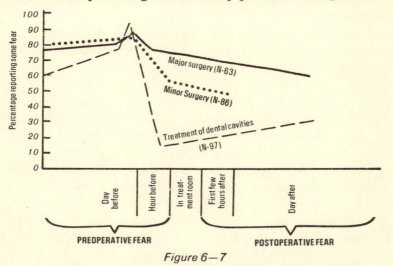

Figure 6—7

Course of anxiety as shown by patients at different times during their treatment (from I. L. Janis, *Psychological Stress*, Wiley, 1958. Used by Permission).

171

Presumably a similar pattern of anxiety occurs in the families of patients. The church leader can bring comfort to anxious people such as these, reminding them that God is present and working even in the midst of stress and anxiety.

Stress in Groups

Groups, like individuals, can also experience and react to stress. Families, committees, church groups, missionary teams, choirs, clubs, and other groups can all have problems in handling stress. "The members of the group may be healthy as individuals, and each may possess outstanding abilities, training, and skills. Yet the group may have difficulty in coping with even mild stresses" (Torrance, 1965, p. 139).

A group experiences stress when unfamiliar or unexpected circumstances threaten the central values of the group members. Militant student activists threaten the existence of the university when they advocate "free speech" and demand the "right" to administer the institution. Many church groups have collapsed—or at least divided—when new doctrines or standards have been introduced by some members of the congregation.

As with individuals, group reactions depend somewhat on the intensity of stress (see Figure 6-6). When the stress is mild or of relatively short duration, the group members draw together. There is greater cooperation, less concern about prestige differences, increased tolerance for one another, and often a willingness to sacrifice personal goals for the good of the group. When the stress gets intense, however, the group may collapse into bickering, apathy, or disintegration.

To prevent a group from breaking down, the members must maintain *affect,* or a concern for each other, there should be a clear *power* structure, *communication* must be maintained, and there must be continued dedication to the group *goals* (Torrance, 1965). Table 6-1 lists a number of questions dealing with affect, power, communication and goals. In strong groups, the answer to these questions would mostly be "yes." "No" answers indicate that a group is weakening and needs to be strengthened.

172

Table 6—1

Issues in groups stability. The more "yes" answers to the following questions, the more stable the group. "No" answers indicate that the group is weakening.

AFFECT

1. Do members of the group help each other without being asked?
2. Do members willingly teach each other when the group is learning new skills?
3. If a member of the group is ill, in trouble, or does not know what to do, are the other concerned?
4. Is the joking in the group good-natured rather than vicious?
5. Do group members get over disagreements easily?
6. Are the members able to disagree without losing their tempers and becoming emotional?
7. Are all members included in activities? Do all members share in the peculiar language and jokes of the group?
8. Do all members want to remain in the group?
9. Do few accidents occur in the group?
10. Do members have pride in the group?

POWER

11. Does someone take responsibility for organizing the activities of the group?
12. In a large group, is authority distributed among members rather than retained by the leader?
13. Is control maintained easily?
14. Can the group make decisions without undue delay?
15. Do group members carry out decisions, requests, and commands willingly?
16. Does the leader back up those to whom he delegates authority?

COMMUNICATION

17. Does the leader keep the group well briefed? Does he pass on information from interdependent groups, superiors, and the like?
18. Do all members, from top to bottom, keep others informed as to what they are doing?
19. Do the members of the group influence one another a great deal?
20. Do members consider one another's opinions? Are disagreements permitted?

GOALS

21. Do the members of the group know what they are trying to do and how they can achieve their goals?
22. Do the members of the group accept learning assignments and exercises? Do they see the reasons for this kind of learning, thinking, or practice?
23. Do group members focus their energies on getting the job done, rather than dissipating their energies in interpersonal squabbles, griping, pursuit of personal pleasures, or the like?
24. Are group members really trying to accomplish something rather than being concerned only about meeting requirements?
25. Do group members avoid short-cuts that would get them out of work or training?
26. Are members on time for scheduled activities?
27. Do group members play the game rather than complain that certain activities are unnecessary?

Adapted from *Constructive Behavior: Stress, Personality and Mental Health* by E. Paul Torrance. © 1965 by Wadsworth Publishing Company, Inc., Belmont, California, 94002.

How are groups strengthened? According to Dr. Paul Torrance, the psychologist who composed the questions in Table 6-1 and one who has done considerable research on the problem of stress, the most important step is awareness. When members know of the threats to group stability, there is increased willingness to work on the problems in an effort to keep the group functioning.

Stress in the Ministry [1]

The minister and his family are not immune from the stress and anxiety that we have been discussing in this chapter. On the contrary, the ministry is characterized by a number of unique stresses. These include:

Social Isolation The young Christian is applauded when he first declares his intention to enter the ministry and often respected as a leader when he later enters the pastorate. Like all people in public life, however, the minister has a lonely job. He lives in a fishbowl where he is carefully watched by the congregation. The pastor and his wife must listen to the problems of others—for this is an important part of their ministry—but there are few human ears to whom they can confidentially express their own discouragements and uncertainties.

Excessive Demands A pastor is expected to fulfill many roles: preacher, evangelist, youth leader, saint, scholar, father, counselor, parish promoter, community problem solver and (in many places) janitor, secretary and chaffeur —to name a few. His wife, who often has had little or no theological training, is frequently expected to speak, make calls and generally fulfill the functions of assistant pastor. Even the pastor's children feel demands when they are expected to be well-behaved, strongly spiritual and present at all meetings of their age group. It is not surprising that a "sense of personal inadequacy" tops the list of reasons why men leave the ministry (Jud, et. al., 1970). Too often, the many demands of his job rob the pastor of necessary time with God, interfere with family fellowship and bring feelings of anxiety, discouragement and inferiority when there is criticism or when things are not running smoothly.

Financial Strain   Several years ago, *Time* magazine noted that the pay of ministers is now becoming respectable. Not only are salaries rising, the article suggested, but there are numerous added benefits like free housing and free utilities. In spite of this, however, the pastor's salary is still very low. Many receive an annual income of less than $5,000 and few exceed a salary in excess of $10,000, in spite of their extensive education and very long hours. Between 1963 and 1968 the cost of living rose fourteen per cent in the U. S.—ministers salaries rose seventeen per cent, but the salaries of other professions rose from twenty-two per cent to forty-nine per cent (Mills, 1969). Even with fringe benefits, the pastor's family in many cases is forced to struggle along on a very tight budget. This can cause strain within the family circle and concern over the pressures of meeting financial obligations in a manner that will maintain one's "good Christian witness."

Administrative Pressures   Church affairs must be conducted in an orderly manner (I Corinthians 14:40) and a pastor is in overall charge of a big business. He is often responsible for efficient handling of a large budget, a detailed program and a church board that may not always be sympathetic or supportive. Since few seminaries or Bible schools provide training in good business methods, the pastor must struggle along as best he can, hoping that some members of the church will be able to give good business advice. All too frequently, these administrative demands take up so much time that the pastor is forced to reduce his study and prayer time. Increasing frustration develops as men who feel called to minister spend increasing amounts of time as administrators.

Professional Competition   Competition is a characteristic of our North American way of life. Children compete for grades and athletic trophies. Merchants compete for sales. Politicians compete for votes. Military, professional and business men compete for advancement and increased assurances of security. It is hardly surprising then, that this attitude seeps into the ministry. Large building programs, large churches, large membership lists, large crowds, large budgets or large numbers of "decisions" sometimes become status symbols and objects of competition among pastors. Too often, denominational meetings are characterized by strivings between factions. Such competition not only detracts from the main function of the pastorate but is also certain to produce frustration, jealousy and continued pressure in the lives of the competitors and their families.

Psychological Tensions   Thus far we have considered pressures that the pastor meets in dealing with people and situations around him. In addition within the pastor himself are tensions that can be very stressful.

Discouragement, for example, is common among all Christians. It is especially easy for the pastor to get depressed when he considers the task that he is called to perform, the lethargy of so many Christians and the apparent lack of results.

Feelings of inadequacy, while common among pastors, present a special problem for the pastors' wives who rarely have any seminary or other training to prepare them for their roles.

Guilt sometimes arises because the pastor and his family are expected to be Christian leaders and examples. Like other Christians, however, they are tempted to sin, and sometimes—perhaps frequently—they yield to these temptations. This easily leads to strong guilt feelings and a failure to accept God's wonderful forgiveness (I John 1:9).

Anger is a psychological reaction that everyone experiences and a reaction that can often be constructive. In Mark 3:5 we read that Jesus was angry and He must have had the same feelings when He drove the money changers out of the temple. Often anger leads to harsh words, cynical comments, criticism and a lack of cooperation. This only succeeds in producing more and greater tensions. Recently a pastor's wife expressed her feelings when she wrote: "My husband is always too busy and also too tired to spend time with me—much less the baby. I honestly feel that he doesn't care about the baby or me—but is in love with his books and the church and nothing else. I resent this! Why be married?"

Dealing with Stress in the Ministry

Like anyone else, the minister may react to stress with the physical and psychological techniques that were described earlier in the chapter. Like any other person, the minister or members of his family may experience a psychological breakdown or physical collapse if the stress is intense enough. Such breakdowns can be avoided, however, if the minister and the members of his congregation take certain precautions.

Have Regular Physical Check-ups. It is widely recognized in the medical profession that a close relationship exists between psychological and the physical functioning. For this reason, the pastor or the member of his family who is physically "run-down" or who suffers from some undetected physical defect is especially susceptable to pressures from his environment. Periodic physical examinations can lead to the recognition and probable elimination of physical disorders that could increase vulnerability to emotional breakdown.

177

In a very practical memo to pastors, one physician gave six "prescriptions for good health": get regular and vigorous exercise, abstain from nicotine, abstain from alcohol, do not become overweight, reduce salt intake, and avoid fatigue or stress (Dennison, 1969).

Get Organized.   With so many responsibilities and so many demands on his time, the pastor often finds that things begin to pile up.   Instead of dealing with one matter at a time he finds that it is easy to begin worrying about everything at once.   As a result, his concentration is divided and his efficiency is reduced.   As he gets further behind, work gets done in a helter-skelter fashion and the pastor discovers that he is becoming more irritable, more discouraged and more susceptable to the pressures of his environment.

With a life of so many unexpected (and expected) interruptions, it is difficult for a pastor to organize his activities. Nevertheless, the following might be helpful suggestions. First, plan each day.   The pastor should decide what he would like to accomplish in a given time and set out to reach his goal.   This will also involve advance planning as he decides on regular times for study, visitation, consultation, and administration.   It may also involve educating the congregation to the fact that while he is always available for ministering to spiritual needs, the pastor would prefer to discuss church business or other matters during the times when he is available for consultation "in" his study.   In planning time, however, the pastor should not be so rigid that he gets discouraged when he fails to finish all that he had hoped.   This brings us to a second suggestion; set realistic goals.   Moody is reported to have remarked one time that he "would rather put ten men to work than do the work of ten men."   Jesus didn't try to carry on His work alone.   He trained disciples and sent them out as co-laborers. The pastor who feels that he must shoulder all of the responsibility in the church might remember that while this

178

may be the easiest way to get things done, it also encourages laziness and lethargy in his congregation and brings increased pressure into his own life. By setting realistic goals for himself and by encouraging others to help, the pastor obtains greater efficiency and emotional stability through better organization.

Take Time to Relax. Not only should this be done regularly, but the minister should stop feeling guilty because he is "taking time away from the work" to which he feels called. A regular time set aside each week for rest and relaxation enables the pastor to carry on with renewed strength, enthusiasm and efficiency. If possible, at least some of this relaxation time should be spent with the family. This time may not be long, but at least it shows the pastor's wife that she is loved and appreciated, and it shows the children that "although daddy is busy, he still is our daddy."

Find a Sympathetic Friend. At some time, every pastor needs a pastor. The ministry has many stresses and when one's emotions are ignored, they have a way of festering and producing additional psychological problems. By accepting and expressing one's feelings and by sharing one another's burdens, the people in the manse can "let off steam" and learn to see themselves as others see them.

Utilize Spiritual Resources. Ephesians six clearly shows that the Christian is in a serious battle with powerful Satanic forces. He must put on the whole armor of God and this involves being armed with the Word of God, supported by prayer, strengthened by the Holy Spirit and constantly alert. Like any busy professional man it is easy for the pastor to become so engrossed in the cares of his occupation that he spends less and less time with his Lord. The quiet time can easily become a daily guilt-relieving ritual, rather than a vital time of strengthening through fervent prayer

179

and close involvement with the Word of God. Pastors need to remind themselves—as they remind their congregations—that the man who is too busy to study and spend time in prayer, is too busy!

The minister and his family should not shoulder all of the responsibility for dealing with pastoral pressures. The members of the congregation have a Christian responsibility to help the pastor as he faces the demands of the ministry to which he has been called. If church members would engage in the following, the pastor would be strengthened, his ministry would be more effective, the congregation would reap the benefits, and the church of Jesus Christ would take another surge forward.

Pray for the Pastor. The New Testament contains many examples of the power of prayer. This power is still available and the pastor who is backed by a praying congregation, will have a more efficient and spiritually enriched ministry (see Eph. 6:18).

Recognize the Problems of the Ministry. Even very active church members often fail to recognize the burden that is faced by the average pastor. It is almost impossible for the pastor to talk openly about stress in the ministry—for he is sure to be misunderstood. Lay church leaders can alert the congregation to these problems, however, and this can hopefully lead church members to be less demanding and more considerate of the pastor and his family.

Remove Some of the Pressures. In Acts six we see murmuring in the church. Apparently the church leaders had become so busy that they could not meet all of their obligations. The problem was solved when church members took over some of the pastoral responsibilities.

By recognizing the pastor's strengths and helping where he is weak, the church members can do much to eliminate murmuring and help the pastor in his ministry. "Our pastor isn't very good at visiting and making calls," a lady once remarked to the author, "but his sermons are well prepared — and there are others of us in the church who can do the calling." This is the spirit of understanding and cooperation which reduces pastoral tensions.

Provide an Adequate Salary. The pastor should not be required to live on a salary which is below the average of his congregation. A good guideline in fixing the salary would be as follows. Invite all members of the church board to anonymously write their annual salary (before taxes) on a slip of paper. These figures could be added and averaged to arrive at a suitable salary for the pastor. There is a good chance that he would get a deserved raise!

Respect the Pastor's Personal Life and Study Time. Good sermons are not prepared in the midst of constant interruptions. The church member including the lay leader should try to avoid disturbing the pastor when he is studying, should encourage the pastor to take at least one day off every week, and should try to respect the pastor's privacy.

Stress and the Church

Groups and individuals within the church, including the pastor and his family, are all influenced by the stresses of modern living. The church leader who wants to understand behavior and work effectively with people must know something about the causes of stress and the ways in which people commonly react to the problems of life. Such knowledge enables the church to (1) better understand and accept the actions of people who are experiencing stress; (2) identify individuals who are having difficulty in handling stress; (3) more effectively counsel with such people; (4) minister more helpfully to families at times of illness, death, and other crises; and (5) more easily handle the stresses which come into his own life and family.

Summary

Anxiety and psychological stress are almost universal in our modern western society. When a situation hinders us, makes a task more difficult, or causes us to fail, we experience stress which is accompanied frequently by feelings of anxiety.

Most stress occurs when we are frustrated, in the midst of conflict or under some kind of pressure. The way people respond to these difficulties depends somewhat on the severity of the stress, but there are almost always both physical and psychological reactions.

Stress and anxiety is not confined to individuals such as church members. Groups sometimes come under stress and so do pastors and their families. When we know something about the causes of stress and typical stress reactions we are better able to minister to the people with whom we come in contact.

NOTES

Chapter One

1. Those psychologists who study behavior that can be easily seen, and those who are concerned about less observable thoughts and feelings, use different study techniques and often appear to be dealing with different subject matters. The conclusions of these different researchers sometimes conflict and this may give the impression that psychology is hopelessly divided into factions. While a unified psychology does not exist today, future unity is a goal toward which some psychologists are now working (see Kendler, 1970).

2. Dates in parentheses refer to the year in which the reference was published. References are listed in detail in a separate section.

3. The Missions Advanced Research and Communication Center, 919 W. Huntington Drive, Monrovia, California, 91016, is an excellent example of the application of computer technology to work of the church. For further information, see Dayton (1969). Note also the Christian Research Institute's Project SENT/East, 116 Surrey Drive, Wayne, N. J., 07470).

1. The drug was quickly removed from the market. Thalidomide children are now being treated in special rehabilitation centers where they learn to use artificial limbs. Because of this treatment, many of these children will live happy, useful lives.

2. It should not be assumed, of course, that these infant problems only arise from maternal stress during pregnancy, but this is one possible cause.

3. The ways in which children learn to think and communicate is a very important issue in modern psychology (DeCecco, 1967; Vetter, 1969; Brown, 1970). A lot of research is now being done on this topic—research which should have practical application for parents and Christian education in the future.

4. Piaget believes that children must grasp the principle of conservation before they can develop the concept of numbers. To study conservation, Piaget designed tests such as the following: Take two glasses, each containing a similar amount of water, say three ounces. Children readily acknowledge that there is an equal amount of water in each glass. Now pour the contents of one glass into a low flat pan, and pour the contents of the other into a tall narrow vase. Do the vase and pan contain equal amounts of water? For those who have learned conservation (the amount "remains the same regardless of the shape") the answer is "yes." For others the answer is "no."

5. It didn't make much difference, however, whether the children who had their names on the roll ever *attended* Sunday school. When the Sunday school members were divided into two groups —those who attended regularly and those who stayed away— there were no differences in behavior. Apparently parents who did a good job in moral training, *enrolled* their children in Sunday school, but didn't insist that they attend.

6. A free pamphlet entitled "When Children Ask About Sex" can be obtained by writing Child Study Association of America, 132 East 74th Street, New York, N. Y., 10021.

Chapter Three

1. Contrary to the opinion of some writers, the author does not believe that the sin of Onan in Genesis 38 refers to masturbation. Onan permitted his semen to be "spilled on the ground," not because he was masturbating, but because during the act of intercourse he did not want his brother's wife to become pregnant (see verses 8-10).

2. The use of drugs by adolescents is an important issue which is discussed in detail in another book in this series.

183

3.   Such people often have a distorted view of prayer. They think
       prayer consists of making personal demands of a divine Santa
       Claus. In most cases they know nothing of prayer as a communion
       with God; an opportunity for thanksgiving, guidance, and comfort;
       a chance for self-examination; and a time for the molding of our
       our desires and our petitions to fit with the perfect will of God.

Chapter Four

1.   How does a church counselor advise a young person in his choice
       of a college? Although opinions vary (and the advice must depend
       somewhat on the student's plans) it is the author's belief that a
       good liberal arts college or state college is best for undergraduate
       education. Then the student who wants specialized training should
       attend a professional school or university. These issues are dis-
       cussed further in a later volume in this series entitled *Restoration:*
       The Psychology of Counseling.

2.   Several writers have attempted to classify contemporary college
       students into more than three categories. One recent study has
       suggested that in place of the "typical college student" we now
       have eight general types: the compliant traditional students, the
       anxious students who are much concerned about the professor's
       opinion of them, the dismayed but hard-working students, the in-
       dependent thinkers who tend to see the teacher as a fellow learner,
       the heros who are trying to make a unique name for themselves,
       the snipers who are overtly rebellious, the attention-seekers, and
       the silent students who sit on the sidelines looking at the professor
       with awe (Ringwald, et. al. 1971).

3.   All of these are mentioned in the Bible: Genesis 1:28, 2:18, 24;
       I Corinthians 7:9; Hebrews 13:4; I Timothy 5:14.

Chapter Six

1.   The material in this section is adapted from an article, written
       by the author and originally published in *the Pastor's Manual,*
       (Collins, 1965).

SUGGESTIONS FOR FURTHER READING

Chapter One

The history of psychology is presented in detail by Boring, *A History of Experimental Psychology* (2nd ed., 1950), but for a more concise approach, see Keller, *The Definition of Psychology* (1937)* and Bromberg, *The Mind of Man: A History of Psychotherapy and Psychoanalysis* (1959).* An historical approach to pastoral care is presented in Clebsch and Jaekle, *Pastoral Care in Historical Perspective* (1964). Skinner, *Science and Human Behavior* (1953)* and Bachrach, *Psychological Research* (1965)* give comprehensive introductions to the scientific aspects of psychology.

The Profession of Psychology (1962) by Webb, gives an overview of the field and discusses in detail such topics as psychology in the universities, clinics, schools, industry and governmental agencies. A booklet by Boneau, Golann and Johnson, *A Career in Psychology* (rev. ed., 1970)* gives more concise information about the profession and is available by writing to the American Psychological Association, 1200 Seventeenth Street, N.W., Washington, D. C., 20036.

For the church leader who wants to keep abreast of trends in pastoral psychology, the journal *Pastoral Psychology** is published monthly (Manhasset, L. I., New York, 11030). The theology is liberal but the psychology is often very relevant to the work of the church.

Chapter Two

There are a number of basic textbooks dealing with child development. *Childhood and Adolescence* (1968) by Stone and Church is the most readable. More scholarly, but less interesting to read, are excellent volumes by Hurlock, *Child Development* (1964), Jersild, *Child Psychology* (1968), and Mussen, Conger and Kagan, *Child Development and Personality* (1969). The problems of young children are discussed in Senn and Solnit, *Problems in Child Behavior and Development* (1968), Clarizio and McCoy, *Behavior Disorders in School Age Youth* (1970), and Wolff, *Children Under Stress* (1969).

* Available in paper back editions.

185

For a brief summary of characteristic behavior at different stages in development, a good summary is provided by Britton and Winans, *Growing from Infancy to Adulthood* (1958).* Spock, *Baby and Child Care* (1957),* and Ilg and Ames, *The Gesell Institute's Child Behavior* (1955)* are inexpensive, practical, and popular guides to the problems and characteristics of children. From a Christian perspective, the church member might be referred to books like Narramore, *How to Understand and Influence Children* (1957) and Brandt and Dowdy, *Building a Christian Home* (1960). *Dare to Discipline* (1970) by Dobson, is a highly recommended treatment of the discipline problem, written by a man who is a Christian and a psychologist who knows what's going on in his field.

Chapter Three

For the reader who wants a better understanding of adolescence, Elizabeth Hurlock's book, *Adolescent Development* (1967) and McCandless, *Adolescents: Behavior and Development* (1970) are both excellent. Together they summarize several thousand research articles in clearly written presentations. An older but briefer guide for parents is by Frank and Frank, *Your Adolescent at Home and in School* (1956).* Gallagher and Harris, *Emotional Problems of Adolescents* (1964) is a guide for ministers and others who "want to understand normal adolescents and their everyday problems." As the title indicates, a book by Goethals and Klos, *Experiencing Youth: First Person Accounts* (1970), is a description of adolescence as reported by adolescents. The survey of Lutheran youth conducted by Strommen, *Profiles of Church Youth* (1963), and the study of Protestant Evangelical teenagers by Zuck and Getz, *Christian Youth: An In-Depth Study* (1968) are valuable sources of information concerning the religious beliefs and practices of select groups of teenagers.

Books by Evelyn Duvall, *Why Wait Till Marriage?* (1965) and Babbage, *Christianity and Sex* (1963)* are clearly written and suitable for teenage reading. One of the best books on the physiology of sex is that of Lewin and Gilmore, *Sex Without Fear* (1965). This is not available in stores, but a pastor or church leader can purchase copies by writing to the publisher: Medical Research Press, 136 West 52nd Street, New York, N. Y.

There are a number of books which give practical advice to youth leaders. *Counseling With Teenagers* by Blees (1968)* and Towns, *Succesful Youth Work* (1966)* are helpful. For the more serious reader, *Counseling the Adolescent* (1967) by Schneiders and others, is a worthwhile book, although it is not written from a religious perspective. Winter and Nuss, *The Young Adult: Identity and Awareness* (1970)* is a collection of articles from psychological journals.

Chapter Four

The "Successful Pastoral Counseling Series," published by Fortress Press, has a number of books dealing with young adulthood. While these are primarily counseling books, they also give information about the nature of the problems of young adulthood. See Harris, *Counseling the Serviceman and His Family* (1966);* Hudson, *Marital Counseling* (1963)*; Kemp, *Counseling with College Students* (1967);* and Terkelsen, *Counseling the Unwed Mother* (1964).*

Campus Gods on Trial (1962), by Chad Walsh, discusses religion on the college campus. For an excellent overview of the current campus situation, see Woodring *The Higher Education in America: A Reassessment* (1968).* Paul Little, *How to Give Away Your Faith* (1966) is a practical guide for witnessing on the campus and elsewhere.

Small's *After You Say I Do* (1968) discusses problems of the young married. The problems of single adults are discussed by Towns, *The Single Adult and the Church* (1967)* and Gleason, *Single Adults in the Church* (1952). For a Christian perspective on military life, written for servicemen, see Combs, *So You're in the Service* (1968).*

Chapter Five

The problems of maturity are considered in a number of fine books. In the Successful Pastoral Counseling Series, Brown, *Counseling with Senior Citizens* (1968)* deals directly with the aged. Since many older people are physically sick and facing death, the church leader might benefit from Scherzer, *Ministering to the Physically Sick* (1968), Bachmann, *Ministering to the Grief Suffer* (1967),* and Scherzer, *Ministering to the Dying* (1967).* The report of a 1961 "White House Conference on Aging," entitled *The Nation and its Older People* (1961)* is available from the U. S. Government Printing Office. For a more detailed account, see Birren, *The Psychology of Aging* (1963). Probably the best work dealing with the older person in the church is Gray and Moberg, *The Church and the Older Person* (1962).* A practical volume, dealing with a specific aspect of work with older persons is Klein, etc. al. *Promoting Mental Health of Older People Through Group Methods: A Practical Guide* (1965).

For a textbook dealing with the whole period of adulthood and focusing on "average" adults, see Bischof, *Adult Psychology* (1969).

187

The material in this chapter is discussed in most general psychology and abnormal psychology books. For the more serious students, Torrance, *Constructive Behavior: Stress Personality and Mental Health* (1965) and Yates, *Frustration and Conflict* (1965)* are good reports, although they are technical in spots. Arkoff, *Adjustment and Mental Health* (1968) has good chapter on frustration, conflict, anxiety, and defense, while Wolff, *Children Under Stress* (1969) discusses the reactions of young people.

For a discussion of anxiety, see Levitt, *The Psychology of Anxiety* (1967)* Goldstein and Palmer, *The Experience of Anxiety* (1963)* gives a number of first hand reports of anxiety experiences.

The problems of the ministry have been discussed by Oates, *The Minister's Own Mental Health* (1961), and Hulme, *Your Pastor's Problems: A Guide for Ministers and Laymen* (1966). An article by McDill (1969) lists a number of references dealing with this topic. For a detailed study of why men leave the ministry see Jud, Mills and Burch, *Ex-Pastors: Why Men Leave The Ministry* (1970).*

BIBLIOGRAPHY

Aldrich, C. K. *An Introduction to Dynamic Psychiatry.* New York: McGraw-Hill, 1966.

Allport, G. W. *The Individual and His Religion.* New York: Macmillan, 1951.

Arkoff, A. *Adjustment and Mental Health.* New York: McGraw-Hill, 1968.

Ausubel, D. P. *Theory and Problems of Adolescent Development.* New York: Grune and Stratton, 1954.

Babbage, S. B. *Christianity and Sex.* Chicago: Inter-Varsity, 1963.

Bachmann, C. C. *Ministering to the Grief Sufferer.* Philadelphia: Fortress Press, 1967.

Bachrach, A. J. *Psychological Research,* 2nd ed. New York: Random House, 1965.

Bealer, R. C. and Willets, Fern X. "The Religious Interests of American High School Youth: A Survey of Recent Research." *Religious Education,* Vol. 62 (1967), pp. 435-444, 464.

Bell, R. and Bell, Helen "Education Helps Parents," *Pastoral Psychology,* Vol. 19 (May, 1968), pp. 27-32.

Bell, R. R. "The Marital Expectations of Adolescents," in J.F. Adams, *Understanding Adolescence* (Boston: Allyn and Bacon, 1968), pp. 272-286.

Benson, D. C. *The Now Generation.* Richmond, Virginia: John Knox Press, 1969.

Berelson, B. and Steiner, G. A. *Human Behavior: An Inventory of Scientific Findings.* New York: Harcourt, Brace, and World, 1964.

Birren, J. E. *The Psychology of Aging.* Englewood Cliffs, N.J.: Prentice-Hall, 1964.

Birren, J. E. "Toward an Experimental Psychology of Aging," *American Psychology,* Vol. 25 (February, 1970), pp. 124-135.

Bischof, L. J. *Adult Psychology.* New York: Harper and Row, 1969.

Blees, R. A. *Counseling With Teen-Agers.* Philadelphia: Fortress Press, 1968.

Boneau, C. A., Golann S. E., and Johnson, M. M. *A Career in Psychology.* Washington D. C.: American Psychological Association, 1970.

189

Bonnell, J. S. "Religion on the American college campus," *Pastoral Psychology,* Vol. 15 (February, 1964), pp. 174 27-30.

Boisen, A. T. *The Exploration of the Inner World: A Study of Mental Disorder and Religious Experience.* New York: Harper Torchbooks, 1936.

Boring, E. G. *A History of Experimental Psychology,* 2nd ed. New York: Appleton-Century-Crofts, 1950.

Bowlby, J. *Maternal Care and Mental Health.* World Health Organization Monograph series No. 2, 1952.

Brandt, H. E. and Dowdy, H. E. *Building a Christian Home.* Wheaton, Illinois: Scripture Press, 1960.

Braun, H. W. "Perceptual Processes," in J. E. Birren, ed. *Handbook of Aging and the Individual* (Chicago: University of Chicago Press, 1959), pp. 543-561.

Bridges, Katherine M. B. "Emotional Development in Early Infancy," *Child Development,* Vol. 3 (1832), pp. 324-341.

Britton, E. C. and Winans, J. M. *Growing from Infancy to Adulthood.* New York: Appleton-Century-Crofts, 1958.

Brown, J. P. *Counseling with Senior Citizens.* Philadelphia: Fortress Press, 1968.

Brown, R. "How Shall a Thing Be Called?" *Psychological Review,* Vol.65 (1958), pp. 14-21.

Brown R. *Psycholinguistics: Selected Papers.* New York: The Free Press, 1970.

Bryan, W. L. and Harter, N. "Studies on the Telegraphic Language. The Acquisition of a Heirarchy of Habits," *Psychology Review,* Vol.6 (1897), pp. 345-375.

Burgess, E. W., Locke, H. J., and Thomas, M. M. *The Family,* 3rd ed. New York: American Book, 1963.

Burney, L. E. "Programs for the Aged," *Public Health Reporter,* Vol. 71 (1956), pp. 1168-69.

Butler, R. N. "The Life Review: An Interpretation of Reminiscence in the Aged," in R. Kastenbaum, ed. *New Thoughts on Old Age* (New York: Springer, 1964), pp. 265-280.

Campbell, D. "Adaptions to the Environment by the New-born Child," *Canadian Psychologists,* Vol. 9 (1968), pp. 467-473.

Cavan, Ruth S., Burgess, E. W., Havighurst, R. J., and Goldhamer, H. *Personal Adjustment in Old Age.* Chicago: Science Research Associates, 1949.

Clarizio, H. F. and McCoy, G. F. *Behavior Disorders in School Age Youth.* Scranton, Pa.: Intext Publishers, 1970.

Cleath, R. L. "Hope in the midst of despair," *Christianity Today,* Vol. 14 (March 27, 1970), pp. 3-5.

Clebsch, W. A. and Jaeckle, C. R. *Pastoral Care ın Historical Perspective.* Englewood Cliffs, N. J.: Prentice-Hall, 1964.

Coleman, J. C. *Abnormal Psychology and Modern Life,* 3rd ed. Chicago: Scott-Foresman, 1964.

Collins, G. R. "Spiritual Catastrophic on the Secular Campus." *Western Workshop,* Vol. 1, No. 2 (1963).

Collins, G. R. "Mental Health in the Ministry," *Pastor's Manual (Fall, 1965), pp. 1-8.*

Collins, G. R. "Student Unrest," in G. R. Collins, ed. *Our Society in Turmoil* (Carol Stream, Illinois: Creation House, 1970), pp. 61-78.

Collins, G. R. "Sorry Virginia—Santa Claus is an idol," *Eternity,* Vol.20 (December, 1969) p. 18.

Combs, L. K., Jr. *So You're in the Service.* Glendale, California: Regal Books, 1968.

Confrey, E. A. and Goldstein, M. S. "The Health Status of Aging People," in C. Tibbitts, ed. *Handbook of Social Gerontology* (Chicago: Univ. of Chicago Press, 196x), pp. 165-207.

Coopersmith, S. *Antecedants of Self-esteem.* San Francisco: W. H. Freedman, 1967.

Culver, Elsie T. *New Church Programs with the Aging.* New York: Association Press, 1961.

Cumming, Elaine, and Henry, W. E. *Growing Old.* New York: Basic Books, 1961.

Davids, A., DeVault, S., and Talmadge, M. "Anxiety, pregnancy, and Childbirth Abnormalities," *Journal of Consultant Psychologists,* Vol.25 (1961), pp. 74-77.

DeCecco, J. P. *The Psychology of Language, Thought, and Instruction.* New York: Holt, Rinehart and Winston, 1967.

Dennison, A. D., Jr. "Physician to Pastor: Golf Isn't Enough," *Christianity Today,* Vol. 13 (January 17, 1969), pp. 5-6.

Dobson, J. *Dare to Discipline.* Wheaton, Illinois: Tyndale House, 1970.

Donahue, Wilma, Orbach, H. L., and Pollak, O. "Retirement: The Emerging Social Pattern," in C. Tibbits, ed. *Handbook of Social Gerontology* (Chicago: Univ. of Chicago Press, 1960), pp. 330-406.

Douvan, Elizabeth, & Adelson, J. *The Adolescence Experience.* New York: Wiley, 1966.

Duvall, Evelyn M. *Why Wait Till Marriage?* New York: Association Press, 1965.

Edwards, M. A. D. "A Review of Some Recent Books on Childhood Religion," *Pastoral Psychology,* Vol. 20 (February, 1969), pp. 50-56.

Eddy, E. D. *The College Influence on Student Character.* Washington: American Council on Education, 1959.

Eisenman, R. "Values and Attitudes in Adolescence," in J. F. Adams, ed. *Understanding Adolescence* (Boston: Allyn & Bacon, 1968), pp. 183-197.

Ellzey, W. C. "Education for the Newly Married," *Pastoral Psychology,* Vol 19 (May, 1968), Vol. 19 pp. 21-26.

Erikson, E. H. *Childhood and Society,* 2nd ed. New York: Norton, 1963.

Erikson, E. H. *Identity: Youth and Crisis.* New York: Norton, 1968.

Fiske, D. W., & Maddi, S. R. *Functions of Varied Experience.* Homewood, Illinois: Dorsey, 1961.

Fleming, T., and Fleming, A. "What Kids Still Don't Know About Sex," *Look* (July 28, 1970), pp. 59-62.

Frank, J. "The Role of Hope in Psychotherapy," *International Journal of Psychiatry* Vol. 5 (1968), pp. 383-395.

Frank, L. F. *On the Importance of Infancy.* New York: Random House, 1966.

Frank, L. K., and Frank, M. *Your Adolescence at Home and in School. The New American Library (A Signet Key Book), 1956.*

Freeman, H. A. *"First Grader's Religious Ideas," School Society,* Vol. 34 (1931), pp. 733-735.

Freud, S. *Basic Writings,* A. A. Brill, ed. New York: Random House, 1938.

Freud, S. *The Future of an Illusion.* Garden City, New York: Doubleday, 1927.

Gallagher, J. R. and Harris, H. I. *Emotional Problems of Adolescence,* rev. ed. New York: Oxford University Press, 1964.

Garrison, K. C. *Psychology of Adolescence* 6th ed. Englewood Cliffs, New Jersey: Prentice-Hall, 1965.

Gesell, A. *Infant Development: The Embryology of Early Human Behavior.* New York: Harper & Brothers, 1952.

Gesell, A., and Ilg, F. L. *Infant and Child in the Culture of Today.* New York: Harper & Brothers, 1943.

Gessell, A. *Child development: An Introduction to the Study of Human Growth.* New York: Harper & Brothers, 1949.

Gesell, A., Halverson, H. M., Thompson, H., Ilg, F. L., Costner, B. M., Ames, L. B., and Amatruda, C. S. *The First Five Years of Life: A Guide to the Study of the Preschool Child.* New York: Harper, 1940.

Gleason, G. *Single Young Adults in the Church.* New York: Association Press, 1952.

Goethals, G. W., and Kloss, D. S. *Experiencing Youth: First-person Accounts.* Boston, Mass.: Little Brown, 1970.

Goldstein, M. J., & Palmer, J. O. *The Experience of Anxiety: A Casebook.* New York: Oxford, 1963.

Gonzales, Mary N. "A Vote for Student Protest," *The Atlantic* Vol. 216 (November, 1966), pp. 112.

Gray, R. M. and Moberg, D. O. *The Church and the Older Person.* Grand Rapids, Michigan: Eerdman's, 1962.

Greenberg, M., Pelliteri, O., and Barton, J. "Frequency of Defects in Infants Whose Mothers Had Rubella During Pregnance," *Journal of American Medical Association,* Vol. 165 (1957), pp. 675-678.

Hall, C. E., Jr. "Some Contributions of Anton T. Boisen (1876-1965) to understanding Psychiatry and Religion," *Pastoral Psychology,* Vol. 19 (September, 1968), pp. 40-48.

Harris, T. A. *Counseling the Serviceman and His Family.* Philadelphia: Fortress Press, 1966.

Harrower, M. R. "Social Status and the Moral Development of the Child," *British Journal of Educational Psychology* (1934), pp. 75-95.

192

Hartshorne, H., and May, M. A. "A Summary of the Work of the Character Education Inquiry," *Religious Education,* Vol. 25 (1930), pp. 607-619, 754-762.

Hattwick, B. W. "The Influence of Nursery School Attendance Upon the Behavior and Personality of the Preschool Child," *Journal Exc. Education,* Vol. 5 (1936), pp. 180-190.

Havighurst, R. J. "Employment, Retirement and Education in tha Mature Years," in I. Weber, ed., *Aging and Retirement* Gainesville: University of Florida Press, 1955) pp. 57-62.

Havemann, E. "The Teen-agers Case Against Parents," *McCall's* (November, 1956), pp. 45f.

Hendricks, H. G. "Unpublished Survey on the Reasons for Sunday School Drop Outs," *Personal Communication* (March 21, 1969).

Hoppe, R. A., Milton, G. A., and Simmel, E. C. *Early Experiences and the Process of Socialization.* New York: Academic Press, 1970.

Hugan, M. D. *The Church's Ministry to the Older Unmarried.* Grand Rapids Michigan: Eerdmans, 1959.

Hudson, R. L. *Marital Counseling.* Philadelphia: Fortress Press, 1963.

Hulme, W. *Your Pastor's Problems: A Guide for Ministers and Laymen.* Garden City, N.Y.: Doubleday & Co., 1966.

Hurlock, E. B. *Adolescence Development* 3rd ed. New York: McGraw-Hill, 1967.

Hurlock, E. B. *Child Development,* 4th ed. New York: McGraw-Hill, 1964.

Hurlock, E. B. *Developmental Psychology,* 2nd ed. New York: Dell Publishing Co., Inc., 1955.

Hurlock, E. B. *Developmental Psychology,* 2nd ed. New York: McGraw-Hill, 1959.

Ilg, Frances L., and Ames, Louise B. *Child Behavior.* New York: Dell Publishing Co., Inc., 1955.

James, W. *The Principles of Psychology.* New York: Henry Holt & Co., 1890.

Janis, I. L. *Psychological Stress.* New York: Wiley, 1958.

Jersild, A. T. *In Search of Self.* New York: Teachers College, Columbia University, 1952.

Jersild, A. T. *Child Psychology,* 6th ed. Englewood Cliffs, N.J.: Prentice-Hall, 1968.

Jones, M. C. and Bayley, N. "Physical Maturing Among Boys as Related to Behavior," *Journal of Education Psychology,* Vol. 41 (1950), pp. 129-148.

Jones, M. C. & Mussen, P. H. "Self-conceptions, Motivations, and Interpersonal Attitudes of Early-and-Late-Maturing Girls," *Child Development,* Vol. 29 (1958), pp. 491-501.

Jud, G. J., Mills, E. W., Jr., and Burch, G. W. *Ex-Pastors: Why Men Leave the Parish Ministry.* Philadelphia: Pilgrim Press, 1970.

Jung, C. G. *Psychological Reflections,* J. Jacob, ed. New York: Harper & Brothers, 1961.

Kagan, J. "His Struggle for Identity," *Saturday Review* Vol. 51 (December 7, 1968), pp. 80-82, 87-88.

Kalish, R. A. *The Psychology of Human Behavior*. Belmont, California: Wadworth, 1966.

Kafner, F. H., and Phillips, J. S. *Learning Foundations of Behavior Therapy*. New York: Wiley, 1970.

Kanter, R. M. "Communes," *Psychology Today* (July, 1970), pp. 53-57, 78.

Kaplan, M. "The uses of Leisure," in C. Tibbits, ed. *Handbook of Social Gerontology* (Chicago: University of Chicago Press, 1960), pp. 407-443.

Kasterbaum, R., and Durkee, N. "Young People View Old Age," in R. Kasterbaum, ed. *New Thoughts on Old Age* (New York: Springer, 1964), pp. 237-249.

Kasterbaum, R. "Elderly People View Old Age," in R. Kasterbaum, ed. *New Thoughts on Old Age* (New York: Springer, 1964b), pp. 250-262.

Keller, F. S. *The Definition of Psychology*. New York: Appleton-Century-Crofts, 1937.

Kemp, C. F. *Counseling with College Students*. Philadelphia: Fortress Press, 1967.

Keniston, K. *Young radicals: Notes on Committed Youth*. New York: Harcourt, Brace & World, 1968.

Kinsey, A. C., Pomeroy, W. B., Martin, E. E., and Gebhard, P. H. *Sexual Behavior in the Human Female*. Philadelphia: Saunders, 1953.

Klein, W. H., LeShan, E. J., and Furman, S. S. *Promoting Mental Health of Older People Through Group Methods: A Practical Guide*. New York: The Manhattan Society for Mental Health, Inc. 1965.

Knight, J. A. "Adolescence Development and Religious Values," *Pastoral Psychology*, Vol. 20 (February, 1969), pp. 39-43.

Korchin, S. J. "Stress," in A. Deutch, ed. *The Encyclopedia of Mental Health*, Vol. 6 (New York: Franklin Watts, 1963), pp. 1975-1982.

Korner, I. N. "Hope as a Method of Copying," *Journal of Consulting and Clinical Psychology*, Vol. 34 (1970), pp. 134-139.

Kuhlen, R. G. *Education for the Aged and for the Aging: Background Generalizations and Recommendations for the Subcommittees on Education and Recreation for the Aged*. Syracuse, N.Y.: Syracuse University Press, 1955.

Kuhlen, R. G. "Aging and Life-Adjusting," in J. E. Birren, ed. *Handbook of Aging and the Individual* (Chicago: University of Chicago Press, 1959) pp. 852-897.

Kuhlen, R. G. "Trends in Religious Behavior During the Adult Years," in L. C. Little, ed., *Wider Horizons in Christian Adult Education* (Pittsburgh: University of Pittsburgh Press, 1962) pp. 1-26.

Kuhlen, R. G., and Arnold, M. "Age Difference in Religious Beliefs and Problems During Adolescence," *Journal of Genetic Psychology*, Vol. 65 (1944), pp. 291-300.

Landis, B. Y. "Religion and Youth," in E. Ginzberg ed., *The Nation's Children* (New York: Columbia, Vol. 2, *Development and Education*, 1960), pp. 186-206.

Langer, T. S. "Normative Behavior and Emotional Adjustment," unpublished doctoral dissertation, Columbia University, 1954. Cited in K. C. Garrison. *Psychology of Adolescence* 6th ed. (Englewood Cliffs, New Jersey: Prentice-Hall, 1965).

Lehman, H. C. *Age and Achievement.* Princeton, N. J.: Princeton University Press, 1953.

Leinwand, G., ed. *Civil Rights and Civil Liberties.* New York: Washington Square Press, 1968, pp. 95-101.

Lenski, G. *The Religious Factor: A Sociological Study of Religion's Impact on Polotics, Economics, and Family Life.* Garden City, N. Y.: Doubleday, 1961.

Levitt, E. E. *The Psychology of Anxiety.* Indianapolis: The Bobbs-Merrill Company, 1967.

Lewin, S. A. & Gilmore, J. *Sex Without Fear,* 2nd ed. New York: Medical Research Press, 1965.

Lidz, T. *The Person: His Development Throughout the Life Cycle.* New York: Basic Books, 1968.

Lindsell, H. "Sex, SIECUS, and the Schools," *Christianity Today,* Vol. 14, (January 30, 1970) pp. 10-13.

Lipsett, L., and Wilson, J. W. "Do Suitable Interests and Mental Ability Lead to Job Satisfaction?" *Educational Psychological Measurements,* Vol. 14 (1954), pp. 373-380.

Martinson, F. M. *Sexual Knowledge, Values, and Behavior Patterns,* unpublished manuscript. St. Peter, Minnesota: Gustavus Adolphus College, 1966.

Maves, P. B. "Aging, Religion, and the Church," in C. Tibbitts, ed. *Handbook of Social Gerontology* (Chicago: University of Chicago Press, 1960), pp. 698-749.

Maves, P. B. and Cedarleaf, J. L. *Older People and the Church.* New York: Abingdon-Cokesbury, 1949.

Illinois: The Dryden Press, 1970.

McDill, T. H. "An Annotated Bibliography on the Mental Health of Ministers and their Families," *Pastoral Psychology,* Vol. 20 (May, 1969), pp. 47-56.

Meehl , P ., et. al. *What then, Is Man?* St. Louis: Concordia, 1958.

Miles, H. J. *Sexual Happiness in Marriage: A Christian Interpretation of Sexual Adjustment in Marriage.* Grand Rapids: Zondervan, 1967.

Moberg, D. O. *Dimensions of Religious Development: Religious Practices,* unpublished paper. St. Paul, Minnesota: Bethel College, 1968.

Mower, O. H. *The Crisis in Psychiatry and Religion.* New York: Van Nostrand, 1961.

Murphy, L. B. *Personality in Young Children.* New York: Basic Books, 1956.

Murphy, L. B. *The Widening World of Childhood.* New York: Basic Books, 1962.

Murray, D., and Coit, M. "Now I Walk Alone," *Saturday Evening Post* (September 16, 1961).

Mussen, P. H. *Child Development and Personality*, 3rd ed. New York: Harper & Row, 1969.

Mussen, P. H., & Jones, Mary C. "Self-conceptions, Motivations, and Interpersonal Attitudes of Late-and-Early-Maturing Boys," Child Development, Vol. 28 (1957), pp. 243-256.

Neugarten, Bernice L. "A New Look at Menopause," *Psychology Today,* Vol. 1 (December, 1967), pp. 42-45, 67-69.

Novak, M. "God in the Colleges," *Harpers,* Vol. 223 (October, 1961), pp. 173-178.

Oates, *W. The Minister's Own Mental Health.* Great Neck, N. Y.: Channel Press, 1961.

Pattison, E. M. "The Development of Moral Values in Children," *Pastoral Psychology,* Vol. 20 (1969), pp. 14-30.

Payne, D. "The Single Woman," *Pastoral Psychology,* Vol. 19 (January, 1968), pp. 41-47.

Piaget, J. *The Language and Thought of the Child.* New York: Harcourt, Brace & World, 1924.

Piaget, J. *The Moral Judgment of the Child.* London: The Free Press, 1932.

Piaget, J. *The Origins of Intelligence in Children.* New York: Norton, 1963.

Piaget, J. *The Child's Conception of Number.* New York: Norton 1965.

Pike, J. A. "Religion and Rebellion," *Psychology Today,* Vol. 1 (August, 1967), pp. 44-49.

Radler, D. H., with Kephart, N. C. *Success Through Play.* New York: Harper & Row, 1960.

Reevy, W. R. "Premarital Petting Behavior and Marital Happiness Prediction," *Marriage and Family Living,* Vol. 21 (1959), pp. 349-355.

Remmers, H. H., Drucker, A. J., and Christenson, H. T. *Courtship Conduct as Viewed by High School Youths.* Purdue Opinion Panel X, No. 2 (Report no. 27), 1950.

Remmers, H. H., & Randler, D. H. *The American Teenager.* Indianapolis: Bobbs-Merrill, 1957.

Resist. "A Call to Resist Illegitimate Authority," published by Resist, Room 4 764 Massachusetts Avenue, Cambridge, Mass. Reprinted in G. Leinwand, ed. *Civil Rights and Civil Liberties* (New York: Washington Square Press, 1968), pp. 95-101.

Ringwald, B. E., Mann, R. D., Rosenweim, R., and McKeachie, W. J. "Conflicts and Style in the College Classroom: An Intimate Study," *Psychology Today,* Vol. 4 (February, 1971), pp. 45-47, 76-79.

Rosen, E., and Gregory, I. *Abnormal Psychology.* Philadelphia: Saunders 1965.

Scaer, D. P. "The Conflicts Over Baptism," *Christianity Today,* Vol. 11 (April 14, 1967), pp. 8, 10.

Schneiders, A. A. *Counseling the Adolescent.* San Francisco: Chandler Publishing Company, 1967.

Scherzer, C. J. *Ministering to the Physically Sick.* Philadelphia: Fortress Press, 1968.

Scherzer, C. J. *Ministering to the Dying.* Philadelphia: Fortress Press, 1967.

Selye, H. *The Stress of Life.* New York: McGraw-Hill, 1956.

Seyle, H. "Stress: It's a G.A.S.," *Psychology Today,* Vol. 3 (September, 1969), pp. 24-26, 56.

Senn, M. J. E., and Solnit, A. J. *Problems in Child Behavior and Development.* Philadelphia: Lea & Febiger, 1968.

Simmons, L. W. "Attitudes Toward Aging and the Aged: Primative Sociaties," *Journal of Gerontology,* Vol. 1 (1946) pp. 72-95.

Skinner, B. F. *Science and Human Behavior.* New York: Free Press, 1953.

Slocum, W. L. "Some Factors Associated with Happiness in Unbroken Homes," *Family Life Coordinator.* Vol. 6 (1958), pp. 35-39.

Small, D. H. *After You've Said I Do.* Old Tappan, N. J.: Revell, 1968.

Sontag, L. W. "War and Fetal Maternal Relationship." *Marriage and Family Living,* Vol. 6 (1944), pp. 1-5.

Special staff on aging. U. S. Department of Health, Education, and Welfare. *Religion and Aging: A Report of the Problems and Issues Together with the Recommendations and Policy Statements from the White House Conference on Aging,* series number 7, Washington, D. C.: U. S. Government Printing Office, 1961.

Spelt, D. K. The Conditioning of the Human Fetus in Utero. *Journal of Experimental Psychology,* Vol. 38 (1948), pp. 338-346.

Spitz, R. A. "Hospitalism: An Inquiry into the Genesis of Psychiatric Conditions in Early Childhood," *Psychoanalytic Study of the Child,* Vol 1 (1945), pp. 53-74.

Spock, B. *Baby and Child Care.* New York: Duell, Sloan & Pearce, 1962.

Stamats, E. C. The Fulfillment Years. *Pastoral Psychology,* Vol. 19 (May, 1968), pp. 33-36.

Staton, T. F. "Sex Education for Adolescence," in J. F. Adams, ed. *Understanding Adolescence: Current Development in Adolescent Psychology* (Boston: Allyn and Bacon, 1968), pp. 248-271.

Stewart, C. W. *The Minister as Marriage Counselor.* New York: Abington, 1961.

Stewart, C. W. *Adolescent Religion: A Developmental Study of the Religion of Youth.* Nashville: Abingdon, 1967.

Stone, C. P., & Barker, R. G. "The Attitudes and Interests of Pre-menarcheal and Post-menarcheal Girls," *Journal of Genetic Psychology,* Vol 54 (1939), pp. 27-71.

Stone, L. J., & Church, J. *Childhood and Adolescence,* 2nd ed. New York: Random House, 1968.

Strommen, M. P. *Profiles of Church Youth.* St. Louis: Concordia, 1963.

Sullivan, H. S. *Conceptions of Modern Psychiatry.* New York: Norton, 1940.

Super, D. E. *The Psychology of Careers.* New York: Harper & Row, 1957.

Taussig, Helen B. "The Thalidomide Syndrome," *Scientific American,* Vol. 207 (August, 1962), pp. 29-35.

197

Terkelsen, H. E. *Counseling the Unwed Mother.* Philadelphia: Fortress Press, 1964.

Terman, L. M. *Psychological Factors in Marital Happiness.* New York: McGraw-Hill, 1938.

Time Magazine "The Old in the Country of the Young," *Time* (August 3, 1970) pp. 49-54.

Torrance, E. P. *Constructive Behavior: Stress, Personality, and Mental Health.* Belmont, California: Wadsworth, 1965.

Towns, E. "The Church and the Single Adult," *Eternity.* Vol. 19 (October, 1968), pp. 18-19.

Towns, E. *The Single Adult and the Church.* Glendale, California: Regal Books, 1967.

Towns, E. *Successful Youth Work.* Glendale, California: Regal Books, 1966.

Vetter, H. J. *Language Behavior and Communication: An Introduction.* Itasca, Illinois: F. E. Peacock, 1969.

Walsh, C. *Campus Gods on Trial.* New York: MacMillan, 1962.

Webb, W. B. *The Profession of Psychology.* New York: Holt, Rinehart & Winston, 1962.

Weiss, A. D. "Sensory Functions," in J. E. Birren, ed. *Handbook of Aging and the Individual* (Chicago: Univ. of Chicago Press, 1959) pp. 503-542.

Welford, A. T. "Psychometer Performance," in J. E. Birren, ed. *Handbook of Aging and the Individual* (Chicago: Univ. of Chicago Press, 1959) pp. 562-613.

Whitlock, G. E. "Emotional Crisis of Those Facing the Draft," *Pastoral Psychology,* Vol. 19 (April, 1968), pp. 43-48.

Wolff, S. *Children Under Stress.* London: Allen Lane the Penguin Press, 1969.

Woodring, P. *The Higher Learning in America: A Reassessment.* New York: McGraw-Hill, 1968.

Wright, Sara-Alyce P. "Youth Participation in Community Affairs," *Children,* Vol. 6 (1959), pp. 140-143.

Yates, A. J., ed. *Frustrations and Conflicts: Selected Readings.* Princeton, New Jersey: Van Nostrand, 1965.

Zuck, R. B. & Getz, G. A. *Christian Youth: An In-depth Study.* Chicago: Moody, 1968.

INDEX